RABBITS ON REPORT

By the same author

**Pigs in the Playground
Calves in the Classroom
Ducks in Detention**

Rabbits on Report

by

John Terry

C.Biol, M.I. Biol, Cert. Ed., M.I. Hort., F.R.Ag.S., F.R.S.A.

with illustrations by John Garbett

First published 2001

Text copyright © John Terry
Illustrations © John Garbett
1 3 5 7 9 10 8 6 4 2

All rights reserved. No part of this publication may be reproduced,
stored in a retrieval system, or transmitted, in any form or by any
means, electronic, mechanical, photocopying, recording or otherwise,
without prior permission of the publisher.

ISBN 0-9541741-0-0

Published by John Terry in association
with Farming Press.

Farming Press books and videos are available to order in UK from
PO Box 76, Bridlington,
East Yorkshire, YO15 3YJ

and distributed in North America by
Diamond Farm Enterprises,
Box 537, Bailey Settlement Road,
NY13607,USA

Printed and bound in Great Britain by Lavenham Press,
Lavenham, Suffolk.

Contents

Introduction   1
1. Fire!!   7
2. The Case Of The Missing Bicycle   31
3. A Cast Of Hundreds   39
4. Milk Fever And Disaster   57
5. It's Enough To Make A Bishop Swear   63
6. Dipping Time   81
7. A New Heifer Arrives   95
8. National Curriculum   111
9. Keeping The School Farm Up And Running   119
10. Community Spirit And Too Much Barley   131
11. The Royal Visit   141
12. Our Rabbits Go Missing   157

Introduction

Farming and teaching are not the easiest careers in the world but I have happily managed, over the years, to combine the two.

I have always been interested in animals. As a boy I kept an assortment of pets, I enjoyed watching wildlife and I helped my parents in the garden. But I was especially fascinated by anything to do with farming. Even the muckiest of jobs held a charm for me.

My holidays and weekends were spent helping my uncle and aunt who managed a farm at Twycross in Leicestershire, owned by an old lady called Mrs Inge. After her death the estate passed into the hands of Lord Clifton, her nephew. He expanded the farming enterprise and bought three neighbouring farms, which then totalled 500 acres. Keeping 180 cows, a large beef unit, sheep and also growing wheat and barley meant there was plenty for me to do and learn. As I grew older I learned how to do more skilled jobs such as milking the cows and driving the tractors.

I left school at eighteen and for one year worked for a local farmer, Mick Hardy. Mick was a rough and ready character who ran a rough and ready farm – if baler twine and a 'bit o' spit' would fix it that was fine with Mick – a total contrast to Lord Clifton's progressive estate. Soon after I started work on Mick's farm he suffered a heart complaint so most of the work was left to me. It's amazing how quickly you learn when there is just you to do the work.

After leaving Mick's farm I completed a three-year specialist rural studies course at Worcester College of Higher Education to qualify as a rural studies teacher. Rural studies is the study of the countryside and how we use the countryside. It can be divided into three main areas, ecology or environmental studies, agriculture and horticulture. After leaving college I needed to find a permanent full-time teaching post. I didn't have to look far because I applied for and was given the post as head of the rural studies department at my old school in North Warwickshire.

It was a comprehensive school with about 950 pupils aged from twelve to sixteen. Head of the rural studies department was a very grand title as the department consisted of an old mobile classroom, textbooks dating back to 1939, an acre of land which was a positive wilderness and fifteen lads. They were all 'less able' students and six of them had criminal records. It was a veritable thieves' kitchen and I was Fagin.

Introduction

Warwickshire County Council gave me only £100 to spend. Even in those days £100 didn't stretch very far and I wanted to set up a school farm and gardens complete with livestock, vegetables, flowers, fruit. greenhouses, a pond and a wildlife area. But by looking around the jungle I had inherited I could see this would have to be a dream for the future.

Our first job was to clear the weeds and then introduce the livestock. I started with two Friesian bull calves called Pinkie and Blackie. It was at this point, I realise now, that I also started my career as the biggest scrounger of all time. As the department grew more students became interested, not just the 'less able' ones but students of all abilities. I introduced CSE and O level examinations and later GCSEs. Over 600 students a week were taking the subject by the early 1980s. The 'digging department' had come into its own.

I managed to build up a rural studies department that we could be really proud of but it didn't come easy, we had lots of stories and adventures as the years passed.

We constructed a duck pond with concrete that, unknown to us, had been stolen and I could have been prosecuted for receiving stolen goods. We took two pigs to the local abattoir and on the journey there the van caught fire, so we almost had roast pork before we got to the abattoir. Another pig escaped into the home economics room where the school inspectors were having their tea and left his calling card on the floor.

When I managed to get plans passed for an extension to our pig building, we started building with the help of a parent who turned out to be a drunk. Then I had a student who thought migration was when his mother got a thumping headache.

We also managed to upset the local bus company. One of my money-making schemes was to sell the by-product of the livestock to the parents for 20 pence a bag. They were supposed to fetch it in their own transport. One lad decided to take his home on the bus. The bus braked suddenly, the bag fell off the rack and burst, spilling its contents on to a lady passenger who promptly hit him on the head with her brolly. The transport manager of the bus company was, to say the least, a little put out by it. Another group of students delivered some barrowloads of manure, unfortunately to the wrong house, and tipped it on to a prize lawn.

We had a ram who shot straight through the greenhouse, breaking no end of glass, and escaping with only a small cut on his nose – we later called him James Bond.

Two of our sheep escaped and were returned to school in the back of a police Panda car at 1.30am. They had gone walkabout. Unfortunately the constable had thrown his hat into the back seat of the car and Tessa and Tina, two of our pedigree ewes thought, 'Oh thank you very much, just what we need' and used it as a convenience, depositing about an inch of pungent yellow liquid in the bottom.

A Kerry Hill ram who was very greedy nearly killed himself eating damsons – we later called him Harry the Hoover.

Gregory, our gander, miraculously helped catch a burglar and thus actually saved the school some money.

We had a very poorly ewe called Jenny. When all else failed I gave her some elderberry wine and after a hangover she made a perfect recovery.

Three calves actually entered a classroom where English was being taught – bringing mayhem and chaos to the lesson.

Ruby, one of our pedigree goats, ran riot at the Summer Fayre causing great embarrassment by almost wrecking the stalls.

One of my students, Nicholas, took some of our ducklings into his detention. Fearing that if he left them they would get cold he transported them in his pocket. They started making a noise, which upset the teacher, and brought the detention to a halt – in fact we had ducks in detention.

When we had a problem with mice, the rodent officer who came was a lady who was terrified of the creatures.

Introduction

One of my students, Anthony, threw a lamb's tail at her. Thinking it was a mouse she screamed and fled the premises, screeching away in her car. No wonder the headmaster kept saying, 'I wish I taught at a normal school Mr Terry.'

All of those stories are true and really happened at the school where I taught from 1974 until 1990.

By 1990 we really had got a department of which we could be proud. By then I had plenty of good students producing excellent work with first-class examination passes.

Our one-acre estate was bulging at the seams. We had really well laid-out flower gardens with roses, a large heather garden and lots of bedding-out plants, hanging baskets and tubs galore. We had two ponds, one for our ducks and the other for wildlife.

As well as the ducks we had many more animals, including up to 85 sheep and lambs. Many of the sheep were pedigree Kerry Hills and we had to rent land to keep them all on. We owned a Jersey cow, which came from the Queen's royal farm at Windsor. She was called Windsor Coronets Crystal 6th. We had kept her since she was a baby calf. She had now grown up and had produced calves of her own. We also kept a few crossbred calves – Hereford x Holstein Friesians. We kept two milking pedigree British Alpine nanny goats, who usually gave birth to twins each year. Four pigs at a time were kept – we sold them at about eighteen weeks old as half-pigs for freezers. This meant we took the farmer's profits and the butcher's profits. Parents and staff were keen to take these half-pigs and all profits made were ploughed straight back into the school farm.

We kept about twenty hens – selling the eggs to staff – a gander and two geese, lots of bantams, rabbits and guinea pigs as pets. These were invaluable in teaching the children to have respect for animals. We even had a pet fox at one stage – an orphaned cub that we reared up and saved from certain death.

The Kerry Hill sheep were the most famous of our stock. We would take them to up to seventeen shows a year, travelling about 3,500 miles. We won many prizes including firsts and championships at the Royal Show at Stoneleigh and in 1986 actually won 102 prizes.

I didn't have time for holidays and weekends off but I enjoyed what I did so much I didn't want to be away from it.

Chapter One
FIRE!!

On Friday nights, when the school week was over, it was customary for me to meet friends for a drink. One Friday night in October Richard Jonas and I were enjoying our regular pint at the Black Horse and the talk, as usual, was about farming.

'My mother is trying to get my father to go on holiday,' he said.

'So what's new?' Graham Wilson almost choked on his beer. 'She's been trying for as long as I can remember.'

'I know. He hasn't been away for twenty-seven years,' Richard replied.

'Good grief, John that beats your record,' Graham said, turning to me.

'I've had a few Saturdays and Sundays off,' I replied defensively.

'Ah, that's not the same though, is it? When did you last have a proper holiday? And I mean a proper holiday. You know, the Grand Tour or the World Cruise. I bet they're missing you on the Canberra.'

'My last proper holiday was seventeen years ago and it wasn't on the Canberra,' I replied.

'Well, there you are you see. Seventeen years is a long time but twenty-seven? Now that would take some beating.'

'I'm not going to try,' I assured him.

'I should hope not,' remarked Graham.

'I might go away for a week next year,' I added.

'Yes I'm sure, I noted the "might", you'll go away next year and knowing you, you'll take all the sheep with you as well,' laughed one of them.

'Will they have to have a passport each?' The question set everyone off into hysterics.

'So what did you father say?' asked Graham when the merriment had finally subsided.

'What do you think? He doesn't want to leave the farm but Mum's getting a bit persistent. She got some holiday brochures from town and seems determined to go to Jersey for a fortnight,' said Richard.

'I'll bet any man in this room a fiver he doesn't go. He's so damn stubborn. He works hard enough all year on the farm – he really deserves a holiday, so does your mother, can't he see that?' said Graham.

'Well don't tell me, try telling him,' retorted Richard.

The following week we were all at our same table when Graham brought up the subject of holidays again.

'So what's the latest on the holiday front then?' he asked. 'Are they going to Jersey?'

'Are they heck!' Richard replied. 'My mother was trying to persuade him again the other night. At first he just sat there and said nothing, then out of the blue he brought out a book he had actually sent for. He said he wasn't going to Jersey in some fancy hotel and then he started showing his book off. It was for farm holidays in Great Britain.'

'Never!' Graham gasped in disbelief. 'He doesn't really want to stay on a farm does he?'

'Yes, preferably his own,' Richard nodded. 'My mother went "spare". I've never seen her so mad. It took us two hours to scrape her off the ceiling. She was livid. But she's adamant he's not getting away with it this year. She's really digging her heels in.'

'You can't blame her. You can just see him though, can't you, comparing milk yields and talking about tractors and fertilisers. That's not a holiday,' Graham remarked.

'That's exactly what my mother said so after a lot of argy bargying and grumbling they've compromised and they're going to stay with her brother in Sussex.'

'It'll be Jersey next year, you see. He'll get a taste for the good life,' I said.

'No chance, you know him as well as I do John.'

'Come on, truth now, are they really going to Sussex?' asked Graham.

'Yes, no kidding,' Richard confirmed.

'For a fortnight?' I asked.

Richard looked at me as if he thought I was mad.

'Don't be silly. A fortnight away from his beloved farm is like a living death to him. No! Five days is all he will agree to but at least it will get him off the farm and off my back.'

'You'll be in charge then.'

'I certainly will and I can't wait,' he replied. 'At long last I'll be my own boss, even if it is only for a week. I wish they were going for a month. There would be some changes made around the place then I can tell you,' he said conceitedly. Little did he know how prophetic his words would turn out to be.

Another week passed and once again we were indulging in a spot of elbow bending.

'They've gone,' announced Richard.

'Really?' Graham looked in amazement at Richard, his glass hovering somewhere between tabletop and face.

'Yes. Finally got rid of him at 7.30 this evening.'

'Was your dad very worried about anything?' Graham asked.

'Anything and everything. You should have seen him. Clucking around like an old hen he was. He did a tour of the farmyard three times checking everything. It took him an hour and a half, which made them late starting off. Mother sat in the car shouting at him and getting hot under the collar. When he finally drove off down the lane he hadn't been gone two minutes and back he came – to check the calf pen door was bolted. Can you believe that? I bet they weren't speaking by the time they got to the end of the lane.'

'Has he left you his instructions?' I asked.

'Instructions? Instructions! I've got instructions for instructions, all written down as well. His parting words to me were, and I quote ... "As soon as I leave this farmyard the place goes to pot. Don't let me down son." He hadn't even been anywhere then,' said Richard, doing a first-class imitation of his father.

'Well, you're a big lad now, Richard. I'm sure you'll cope all right. You're born and bred to it.'

'And he's on solid foods now,' said Graham. 'Of course he'll cope. Have faith, my boy.' He patted Richard on the shoulder.

The rest of the evening was spent in very pleasant

conversation. Mine Host of the Black Horse kept an excellent cellar and we made the most of it, leaving when the barmaid said that much as she enjoyed our company she had certainly had enough of it for one evening and would we kindly vacate the premises before she had to resort to a modicum of Tae Kwon-do and throw us out with the empties. We, being peaceable fellows, left at just after 11pm.

I had certainly had a very busy day and was dog tired, I could hardly keep my eyes open and so it was that 11.30pm saw me under the duvet and straight to dreamland. I was roused at 2.15am by the jangling of the telephone. I answered it on auto pilot.

Before I could speak a voice at the other end said, 'Hello John, it's Richard Jonas here'.

He sounded rather strange.

'Someone's set fire to our stack of big round straw bales and it's going like the bloody clappers. Can you come and help me, please? Now?'

'Yes of course I can,' I replied, still in a daze.

'I could do with some of your pupils too,' he said.

That brought me back to the land of the living.

'You can forget that Richard. It's out of the question.' I couldn't get children out of bed at this hour. They would love it but the parents and the Education Committee might take a different view. 'I tell you what though, I might be able to get three lads who have just left school to help.' I continued.

'Oh John, I wish you would. I need all the help I can get.'

'Leave it with me, I'll see what I can do.'

In less than three minutes I was dressed and letting myself out of the house. It was a dry night and there was a strong wind blowing.

Just what we need, I thought. The old adage says 'it never rains but it pours'. Correction: 'it never rains when it's needed'. It was bitterly cold too so I went back inside for my coat. I knew we weren't in for a cosy night. Fortunately the field where my three former pupils were supposedly camping was only a couple of minutes away and I thought it worth a try to go and see if they were there. They had left school but had visited me on the previous Wednesday; it was then that they had told me they were camping out on Friday and Saturday night on a neighbouring farm. I knew the field and quickly parked my car in the gateway on the side of the road. I ran down the field in the pitch dark. People who live in towns don't realise how dark the countryside is; there are no streetlights in fields. Suddenly the small tent came into view. What a relief. All was quiet; obviously all three lads were asleep, as I should have been. I didn't want to startle them but desperate situations merit desperate actions so I shouted:

'James, Craig, Russell. Wake up. There's a fire at Jonas's farm.'

Three sleepy, sloe-eyed heads emerged from the tent.

'What's up?' asked Craig.

'Are you drunk, sir?' asked James.

'Certainly not. Come on, you're needed.'

'I was fast asleep' moaned Russell.

'So was I,' I said and explained to them again. Within minutes they were fully dressed and raring to go.

They were three good lads, all very interested in farming but although all three were in full-time employment, sadly none were in agriculture. James worked for a firm making school furniture, Craig worked for a builder and Russell for a local plumber. They were strong, healthy specimens, not afraid of hard work, entirely trustworthy and reliable.

Once in my car it was toe hard down and we raced for the farm. Halfway there we could see the ominous orange glow in the night sky and the buildings silhouetted in stark relief against the flaming backdrop.

'Oh well, look at that. It's a good blaze, sir.'

It certainly was.

As we got closer we could see the flashing blue lights of the fire engines and police cars. I parked on the grass at the bottom of the drive. I thought this the most sensible thing to do as that way we wouldn't hinder the firemen and neither would I have to witness my pride and joy blowing into a thousand fragments.

The four of us ran along the straight farm drive. I could see Richard standing at the back door of the house talking to a fireman. There were four engines in attendance. I was informed later that this is known as a 'full shout' – where every appliance is in attendance. I was unsure how Richard would react. Would he be upset or in a flaming temper? I tried to read his face but he spoke first.

'Thank God you're here John.' He was shell-shocked.

'I wish now we had set fire to the straw in the field like Bert Biggins did,' he said dryly. 'It would have been a lot less trouble.'

He was a very unhappy man but he had tried to make a humorous comment. I tried to respond. 'If I'd known it was going to be a big show I could have brought my fireworks and some roasting potatoes.'

Richard gave a sickly smile. I looked around and tried to take in the complete picture but it was one of those scenarios the mind cannot grasp in the first instance. Like an earthquake where hundreds of people have perished, all you can see at first is piles of rubble. Or famine in a third-world country. People starving to death before your eyes but all you can see are skeletal limbs, then it hits home these are human beings. It takes time to absorb the enormity of the tragedy. So it was with me then. I could see the huge flames leaping from the burning buildings, I could smell the smoke, I could feel the intense heat but it was a few moments before it sank in that this was someone's livelihood going up. Richard was of the opinion that it had been deliberately set. Maybe he was right. There was a headcase at large, this wasn't the first farm to have been torched.

About 800 round bales had been stacked at one end and to one side of a four-bay Dutch barn. The barn itself contained silage and on top of the silage were about 1500 conventional bales of straw. The barn and its contents were not on fire but the large bales stacked at the end of the barn were well alight. Bale after bale of straw was catching fire and as every second ticked away the fire pursued its relentless course towards the barn.

One fire engine parked next to the house was pumping water while two other engines were in position to fight the fire. The fourth appliance was parked in order to spray water on some hay in a Dutch barn that was positioned downwind of the fire. Thick acrid smoke billowed over the farmyard and stung our eyes but it was something we had to put up with. It was obvious they were losing it.

The silage barn would be the next to go. The wind was fanning the flames nearer and nearer. If the silage barn did go it probably wouldn't be long before the other Dutch barn followed. Most of the other farm buildings would then be at risk, including the house itself. Sparks and bits of burning straw were blowing in the wind and landing on the other buildings, including the other Dutch barn containing hay. It was a terrifying sight.

I heard a fireman telling Richard there were twenty-six fire fighters at the scene and they were running themselves ragged trying to keep the fire from spreading. It was a mammoth task because the straw and hay were bone dry. The Jonas's farmworker, Desmond, had arrived shortly before me and he was moving the small bales off the top of the silage under the barn, throwing the bales into a trailer. Richard had now jumped on to a tractor and started moving the big bales at the side of the barn with the fore loader attached to the tractor moving three bales at a time. He moved the big bales into a field but unfortunately, in his hurry, he ran over the hose and cut off the water supply. Some firemen quickly found some ramps for the tractor to run over and so prevent the vital supply from being cut off again. He started moving the bales that were furthest away from the fire and moved steadily closer to those that were nearest. The firemen sprayed water on to the bales when they were attached to the tractor and then sprayed the tractor itself; it was a good job the tractor had a covered cab or Richard would have been drenched as well. A hosepipe which had been attached to a bracket on the wall was used to spray water on the other Dutch barn as the firemen that had been operating it had turned their attentions elsewhere.

'If only it would rain,' wailed Richard.

There wasn't much chance of that. Many firemen joined in to help Desmond move the straw bales from the top of the silage. My former pupils helped too. It was a task fraught with danger. The heat was so intense we couldn't get near the actual fire. Nevertheless, the danger of being seriously injured was ever present. A soon as the trailer was full Desmond took it to the field and tipped it up, racing back for another load. Ivor Shorthouse, a neighbouring farmer, then joined us.

'What are you doing up at this time in a morning?' yelled Desmond above the din. It really was a noisy scene. What with the roar of the pumps, the crackling and banging of the fire, running feet and men shouting to each other it was a real cacophony.

'I got up to calve a cow, she produced a fine heifer calf,' he said proudly. 'I put the light off in my building and that's when I saw the red glow. I guessed straight away what was going on so here I am.'

'We're mighty glad to see you as well,' said Desmond.

'Red sky at night, shepherd's delight,' someone said.

'Red sky at night, Jonas's farm on fire,' quipped Desmond and earned himself an evil look from Richard.

Fire!!

'No, red sky in a morning, Jonas's farm on fire,' retorted Ivor.

These feeble attempts at jollity were simply to hide the gravity, and sadness, of the situation. We were all feeling it. If we didn't laugh we would cry. Ivor didn't need telling what to do and knuckled down straight away. He was a good, experienced farmer with enough farming years under his belt to know the score and clear the area in double quick time. He rolled up his sleeves and started moving bales.

Richard's sister Elizabeth arrived and what a bundle of joy she turned out to be. He first 'comforting' words to Richard were 'Whatever will Dad say, Richard?'

Richard didn't answer. She couldn't leave it though.

'He didn't want to go on holiday in the first place and now look what's happened. He's never left the farm for more than a few hours before and the first time he goes away on holiday in twenty-seven years ...' That was it. That was the catalyst that sent Richard over the edge.

'Oh shut up,' he bawled. 'If you can't say anything constructive go home again, go on, clear off. Either that or get your coat off and do something useful like help me save what's left.' I didn't blame him, she'd asked for it.

Suddenly she cried out in panic, 'My horse. My horse.'

'My kingdom for a bloody horse,' mimicked Richard.

'I've got to know if he's all right haven't I?' she snapped.

She stabled her horse at the farm and travelled to look after him.

'He was all right when I saw him earlier on' Richard replied in a calmer tone. Tempers were frayed and nerves shredded.

She ran towards the wooden stable, which was downwind of the fire. Within minutes she emerged with the terrified animal. She had placed a head collar on him and tried to lead him out but the horse wasn't going anywhere. This wasn't the farm he knew. Huge unfamiliar red fire engines, roaring hot flames, choking smoke, loud voices and strange crackles and bangs all added to his terror. He whinnied in fear and suddenly reared up, his front hooves flailing wildly in the hot air. Elizabeth tried to talk to him but her calming words were lost on him. The horse shied again and dragged Elizabeth to her knees. Straining on the halter he reared up again and dragged her back on to her feet. As he came down he landed on one of her feet, she gave a yell of pain and he shied again. For a few minutes it looked as if he would break away but eventually she got him under control and led him away to safety into a small paddock at the rear of the farm, well away from the fire. Once away from the danger he calmed down and began to graze. He was going to be all right.

The smoke in our eyes was stinging painfully and at the back of my mind lurked the dreadful thought that, just suppose another fire had broken out somewhere in another building, with all the commotion going on it could easily have gone unnoticed.

James, Craig and Russell were acquitting themselves very well and I was proud of them. They seemed to have developed an instinct for what to do and were getting on with it without any supervision or guidance from anyone. What a credit they were. Suddenly a fireman came running towards Desmond and me. He had come from the direction of the farm buildings where smoke and sparks were blowing. I thought my premonition about a second fire was about to be realised but the problem was a different kettle of fish altogether.

'Quick' he said, 'the cattle sheds are filling up with smoke. It's blowing in but it's not coming out again.'

Desmond signalled to Richard on the tractor. Richard jumped down and ran towards us.

'What's up?' he asked.

Desmond explained the situation.

'Come on then, let's see if we can get the cattle out. We can drive them into that cubicle shed,' shouted Richard, pointing to the designated shed. Desmond, Ivor, James, Craig, Russell and myself followed Richard to a brick building, the front was open but there were gates which would keep the cattle in. James flung open the gate.

'Six cows due to calve at any minute are in here,' said Richard with concern. We couldn't see them at first because the smoke was so dense. They were valuable Holstein Friesians. Eventually, as our eyes became accustomed to the dimness we just managed to make out their white patches. As we moved to the back of the shed, the hot smoke made my eyes sting and scorched my lungs with every breath. I placed a handkerchief over my mouth and nostrils, shut one eye and squinted awkwardly through the other. Then it was head down and go for it. I needed to run through the thick, black smoke and drive the cattle out. Visions of John Wayne and 'Rawhide' flashed through my mind although I probably looked more like Popeye with my squinty eye or Billy the Kid with the bottom half of my face covered by a mask – actually a handkerchief. I kept quiet about that and didn't say a thing.

Desmond had waited outside and as the cattle barnstormed out he turned them in the direction of the cubicle shed. Once outside I was able to open my eyes properly but the poor cattle were wide eyed with terror and came to a juddering stop in the yard. Their normally peaceful, tranquil yard was transformed into a living replica of 'Dante's Inferno'. The silage barn was well alight, flames thirty feet high shot up into the night sky. The heat was searing and the fire was now nearer the buildings. The cows were not the only ones to feel the fear, you could taste it. We managed to herd the cows into the cubicle shed which was smoke free and, like the horse, once they couldn't see the fire they calmed down. At least the expectant mothers had come through it well and looked placid enough; they were not going to calve that night.

'We'll have to move the calves next,' shouted Richard, indicating the calf shed. 'We can put them in the other cubicle shed.' The calf building was a brick building with individual pens inside and a feed passage running between the pens. It was the same here as it had been in the cow shed, we couldn't see much at all. The calves ranged from a week old to five weeks old. Let out of the pens some of them just stood there bewildered, they hadn't been out of the pens since they had been put in and didn't know what to do or where to go. We had to walk to the back of each pen and drive or push them out. We moved all twenty into the central feed passage but they were difficult to drive out. Some of the older, stronger calves were in front jumping and frolicking, enjoying their new-found freedom but some of the younger ones didn't want to move and so we just pushed them along.

Having got them outside it was a dash between buildings. Where the flames were not lighting up the area it was very dark and some of the calves were running between the buildings while others disappeared behind a row of farm implements. One got so excited it slipped on the wet concrete. Another one got stuck between a wall and a gate but Craig freed it – I was delighted to see he still cared. Eventually we had moved them all and they were safe in the other cubicle shed.

Then the pantomime started: what followed next was a virtual showstopper.

'You know what we've got to move next,' said Richard, running towards the bullpen.

It didn't take much working out – the pedigree bull called Performer. He was a rare size to tangle with. One of Nature's monsters, he was not a gentle giant by any means and not known for his sweet temper. If he said it was Wednesday it was Wednesday. A cantankerous devil at the best of times the Lord alone knew what this night's palaver had done to his disposition. He lived in a brick shed with an open yard attached and he was standing slap in the middle of his private patio. His shed was full of smoke and the yard wasn't much better.

No one could possibly know what was going through that bovine mind at having his sleep disturbed but he stood there, an enormous strong masculine mountain of beef weighing at least a ton and gave us a very lary eye.

'And who, may I ask, is taking him for walkies,' I ventured to ask.

'Well, I could put a rope through his nose ring and try to lead him out but I'm nervous around him and he'd soon pick up on that. We'd probably finish going walk about on the A5,' Richard said. 'Does anyone else fancy their chances?'

There were no takers – which was hardly surprising. You'd need a stockman like Goliath to take him on.

'How about you, John?' Richard asked.

'No thank you. I'd rather not if you don't mind,' I replied.

'Go on Mr Terry, you can do it,' Russell said.

'Well, thank you very much, Russell. It's nice to know you have so much confidence in me. Thanks but no thanks. I'll pass on that one if you don't mind. First and foremost I don't know the bull,' I protested.

'I can soon introduce you,' said Richard, but a little too quickly for my liking.

'Forget it. If anyone's taking him it's you Richard.' I dug my heels in.

'Come on, let's see if we can drive him,' said Richard.

Richard approached Performer cautiously. The bull seemed very surprised to see him at that hour and even more surprised that he was getting so close. The bull snorted and his head went down. Eyeing Richard with great suspicion he watched as he eased his way forward. What was this puny little Homo erectus up to now? Richard edged his way around the side of Performer. Performer's gaze followed him. Even through the smoke I could see the whites of his eyes. He pawed the ground, gave another snort and let forth a mighty bellow.

'Watch him Richard. You know what a mean devil he can be,' called Desmond in alarm.

'I'm watching him all right. Never fear,' Richard replied.

All the time Richard was gradually getting behind the bull. We all moved out of the way. Richard hit Performer on his back but it had no effect, he didn't flinch. He didn't even feel it. I ran to give Richard a hand and the others followed. Once behind him we were comparatively safe from his lethal head. It's not only horns that can kill; there's a lot of pressure behind that heavy skull, enough to crush the life out of a stockman.

First a cowboy, now a matador, I thought. Whatever next? Two careers in one night must be a record.

We got him on the move and he charged forward, then to everyone's dismay he turned left, straight towards the fire instead of right, away from it. Oh terrific, beefburgers all round. Mr Jonas would not have been very pleased if he returned from holiday to find his prize bull had been barbecued.

'After him,' I shouted and Craig hurtled off with Russell in hot pursuit.

'Get behind him,' I yelled.

'We've got to catch him first, sir,' they called back.

Eventually they managed to head him off. He was frightened as well as angry and a frightened, angry bull is a force to be reckoned with. At last the lads managed to turn him in the right direction. I moved well back out of his way; if he charged he could do more damage than a runaway ten-ton truck. We were all running behind him at that point, driving him towards a loose box which was just past the cubicle sheds. However, he got the scent of the cows and although he was scared out of his skin he stopped to look inside. The cows showed no interest in him and we were able to drive him a little closer to the loose box. Richard held the door open. It was then that Performer decided to show everyone just who was boss. He stopped dead in the doorway. He wasn't going in there, it was dark, there was no electric light. The prospect of spending the night in that small dark cell didn't appeal to him at all, especially after being used to the executive suite. Turning, he ran past Richard, who didn't stand a cat in hell's chance of stopping him, and we were off on a merry chase again.

Performer ran towards a gate.

'It's a good job that gate's closed,' said Craig.

Now if that wasn't tempting Providence I don't know what was. No sooner were the words out of his mouth than Performer nudged the gate open and disappeared into a field.

'Oh well, that's it. That's torn it, we shan't see him again,' said Craig.

'Yes we've really lost him now,' declared James.

'No, don't worry, he'll be fine now. Just fasten the gate securely and he won't be back to bother us again,' Richard said confidently.

At that moment two firemen approached us.

'Get that combine harvester out of the shed,' ordered one of them, 'before it blows up and we have another fire.'

Fire!!

There was a loud gasp from Desmond. 'Oh, the combine, your dad's pride and joy. I forgot all about it. I never gave it a second thought.'

'Well you'd better give it more than a second thought and get it moved,' the fireman insisted.

'Don't worry Desmond, you got your priorities in order. You got the livestock to safety and the livestock are far more valuable than any old bit of machinery,' said Ivor.

'But it's not old, it's nearly brand new,' Desmond cried.

'Wait here, I'll go and get the keys from the house,' Richard said as he dashed off.

While he was gone I looked at the barn which was, by now, well and truly alight. The roof was asbestos and it was cracking and caving in – the metal girders supporting it were buckled and mis-shapen.

It was a sorry sight, the firemen were fighting hard to keep it from spreading. Fire, smoke, blue flashing lights and fire appliances are a sight no farmer wants to see on his land.

Richard appeared with the keys to the combine harvester.

'Am I going to lose the next Dutch barn as well?' he asked.

'It's a possibility. Now get that combine out while it's still fairly safe,' instructed the fireman.

Richard jumped up into the driving seat and turned the key. Nothing happened. Richard looked blank. He turned the key again and still nothing happened.

'What's the matter with the damn thing?' he said.

'Ah, I've just remembered, your dad took the battery out of it,' Desmond said.

I thought Richard was going to explode.

'He did what?' he bellowed.

'Took the battery out of it.'

'What the Hell for?'

'In case anyone tried to steal it.'

'You are joking! Who the devil would want to steal a combine? It's not exactly a state-of-the-art getaway vehicle is it? I mean, can you imagine Bonnie and Clyde robbing a bank and using a combine as their means of escape? I don't know where he gets his ideas from.' He was rapidly approaching breaking point.

Desmond climbed on to the tractor and backed it up to the combine. He had the solution, tow it out. Richard found a long heavy chain, attached one end to the tractor and the other to the combine and Desmond towed it to safety. We all heaved a sigh of relief. In a night littered with one crisis after another something had gone right at last.

We returned to the fire.

'If we can just stop the fire spreading to any of the other buildings we'll be satisfied,' said a fireman. His face was black from the smoke and he looked very tired.

'Oh I'm glad someone will be satisfied,' snapped Richard.

'Richard, behave, stop it. They're doing their best and he doesn't deserve that,' I chided.

'No, you're right John. I'm sorry mate.' He apologised to the fireman.

We all started to move some more bales, but it was no use; the heat was too intense to get very close. The fire was ripping its way through the barn and all we could do was stand and watch it burn.

The fire crews had excelled themselves, many of them doing double duty by helping us to move straw bales. It was beginning to look as if they had the fire contained. They had certainly earned their salaries that night. My former pupils had also done themselves proud but they wouldn't expect to be paid for it.

The livestock were safe, the combine harvester was safe and we were all in one piece. Thank the Lord for small mercies. I looked at my watch, it was just after six o'clock. Dawn was breaking as we stood surveying the wreckage. Little wisps of smoke still spiralled up into the thin morning air. I shivered. I could see that the ruins were not the only thing smouldering. Richard was a walking time bomb. He had been quite civil to the lads, Ivor and me, but poor Desmond and Elizabeth had got it in the neck and it would be Heaven help any member of the Jonas's staff or family who crossed his path that morning. Richard went off to do his milking. The fire was almost spent now, all that was left were piles of ash, smouldering timbers and pools of water. I stood looking at the devastation, it was like a scene from the

Fire!!

Blitz. Fortunately the strong wind had died down and was no longer fanning the fire. I hadn't seen it arrive but the fire brigade mobile canteen had arrived in front of the house and the fire crews were being served with food and drinks. I would have killed for a bacon sandwich.

We could be spared now, so I drove the lads back to their tent and went home for a quick breakfast. I caught sight of myself in a mirror and jumped back in alarm. Who was that? My face was so black I looked as if I had just done eight hours down a coalmine.

After a much-needed bath and change of clothes and a quick breakfast I returned to the farm. Soon after I got there Craig, James and Russell arrived on their bicycles looking suitably refreshed. We all joined in Operation Clean Up. We moved straw and ashes, piling it into a trailer, the lads used shovels and forks but I got on better using the tractor and fore loader. It was soaking wet under foot and I very nearly got the tractor stuck on more than one occasion.

Richard returned from milking.

'I'll take over now John,' he said. He worked for about a quarter of an hour before he got the tractor stuck. He was a skilful driver and he needed all the skill he could muster to get the tractor out without being towed. Desmond and my lads placed a concrete block on the back of the tractor to act as a weight and try to stop it happening again but it was too heavy and broke the left arm off the tractor's three-point linkage system. Richard started to swear and the air was just turning a lovely shade of purple when he stopped short as a police car arrived. A constable had come to take a statement from him. They disappeared into the kitchen to complete the paperwork. Now it was daylight, cars had stopped on the nearby roadside and some people had got out to have a look at the scene. I couldn't help wondering if the person who had started the fire, assuming someone had, was among the spectators watching us at that very minute, enjoying it and having a good laugh. It made me ponder on what sort of person gains pleasure from seeing the destruction of someone's lifelong work.

Richard's Uncle Ron arrived with his new telescopic

forklift. A fork on one end grabbed a large amount of still-burning straw, the machine backed out and the straw was placed in a separate heap where the firemen dowsed it with water. By actually moving the fire this way it was methodically extinguished. In fact it was completely out by lunchtime. Ron returned home but not before giving Richard a severe tongue lashing for not sending for him sooner.

We had worked flat out for ten hours with only half an hour's break to snatch some breakfast. Richard tried to tell me several times what had happened but each time he was interrupted either half way or part way through. At last an opportunity to talk presented itself. The ruins surrounded us.

'Look Richard, I know you wanted to make some changes around the place but this is a bit over the top isn't it?' I joked, trying to lighten the moment. 'What happened?'

'I was in bed, fast asleep and thought I was dreaming. Someone was knocking on the door but it got that loud and persistent it woke me up and someone really was knocking on the door. I opened the bedroom window and looked out to see a man hammering on the door and shouting "Mr Jonas, Mr Jonas. Wake up. Your farm is on fire, Mr Jonas," and then bang bang again on the door. I asked him who he was. He said his name was Ray Moore and he lived in the village. "Hurry down, your farm's on fire," he shouted again. I turned away from the window and that's when I noticed my white walls were glowing pink. It took a minute to sink in. I could see the fire but it didn't register that it was our farm going up. Then when it did finally hit home I dashed downstairs to telephone the fire brigade. While they were on their way I got dressed and tried to ring Desmond but he didn't answer so I had to dash over there and almost batter his door down. Do you know there are five people in that house, there's Desmond, his wife and three children and the telephone ringing didn't wake any of them. I reckon they could sleep through an earthquake. Anyway by the time I got back the fire brigade were here so I left them to get on with it while I rang you. The rest you know.'

'The man who raised the alarm, could he be the man who started the fire?' I asked.

'Good heavens no. As soon as he said his name I recognised him. He'd never dream of doing such a thing. He's a really nice bloke,' Richard replied.

'Well there have certainly been a lot of fires in this area.'

'I know. Do you know how many? A policeman told me it was fourteen.'

'Do they have any idea who's responsible?'

'No. They've had a few people in for questioning but they haven't made any arrests yet,' Richard replied.

'Well I hope they catch the culprit soon.'

'So do I because if I catch him before the law does he can cancel any pension plan he might have taken out because I can assure you he won't live long enough to collect it. He would do better to take out a funeral plan instead.'

'Well, it's all over now except the cleaning up,' said Craig, trying to look on the bright side.

'Oh you think so do you? Well the cleaning up is the easy bit. I've got to break the news to the gaffer yet, unless you want to do it.' Richard turned to Craig who quickly declined the dubious honour.

'Come on now, Richard, it's not that bad. He's your father,' I said.

'I know he is but he's still the gaffer and can sack me.'

'He won't do that and you know it. He can't manage without you. Anyway, you're making him sound like an ogre and he isn't,' I said in defence of Mr Jonas senior.

'No. I suppose you're right, but I'm still dreading it.'

Just then Desmond came racing in from the yard.

'It's not all over until the fat lady sings and the fat lady's done a runner,' he gasped, out of breath and sweating profusely.

'Oh what now? What the Hell's going on? I can't take much more. Richard cried in despair.

'It's Performer, boss. He's gone.'

'Gone? How can he be gone and where to? He can't have gone.'

'Come on,' I said jumping to my feet. 'Action stations.'

Richard, Desmond and I ran down to the field where we had last seen Performer, hotly followed by Craig, James and

Russell. We scanned the field anxiously. At first there was no sign of him until an excited cry from Richard pointed us all in the right direction.

'There he is, way over there,' Richard shouted, pointing in the direction of Jim Finney's farm. Performer was two fields away but fortunately still on Jonas's land. We ran, then walked down the fields towards him. None of us had the strength or stamina to run all the way. Besides, we had to conserve what energy we had left as there was still a lot of strenuous work to do. As we approached him we could see he was standing near the boundary of Jonas's land. The boundary was a deep ditch with a hedge on the other side. A tractor, driven by Jim Finney's son Kevin, was cutting the hedge on the Finneys' side and at that moment was rapidly drawing level with the bull. Performer was fascinated, the tractor and machinery was very noisy and was getting closer. He stood there like a fighting bull facing the matador, he didn't like the tractor one little bit and for one dreadful moment I thought he was going to charge. To my relief he changed his mind and jumped into the ditch instead.

Richard was far from pleased.

'You blithering idiot,' he yelled. 'Fancy doing a daft thing like that. That ditch must be eight feet deep and there's water in the bottom you silly beggar.' He really was at the end of his tether.

The ditch wasn't as deep as we first feared and the water came to just below Performer's knees. That was when he spotted us. You could almost hear him thinking, 'Oh no, it's those daft humans from last night.' When it came to a straight choice between us and the tractor it seemed the machinery was the better prospect for giving a snort he suddenly lurched up the bank and pushed his way through the hedge. We didn't see Kevin's face but we did hear the cry of terror as Performer appeared on the other side of the hedge.

'Oh this is just what I need, a hefty compensation claim,' Richard moaned.

Performer had got mud up to his knees and bits of hedge sticking out of his back reminiscent of the short spears used by the picadors in the Spanish bullrings. Once on the other

Fire!!

side he found himself face to face with that confounded contraption that had been tormenting him and to Kevin's horror he charged. Kevin wasn't so much worried as panic-stricken. There was no cab on the tractor so he could easily have been gored. The whole scene reminded me of a rhino charging a Land Rover on the African plains.

If the situation hadn't been so grave it would have been hilarious, like something out of a Carry On Film. The huge black and white beast head-butted the tractor two or three times more. Richard was climbing down the ditch. He was going over to Performer although I don't know what he thought he could do. A charging bull is a law unto itself. One saying to be heeded is 'Don't mess with the best' because when the 'best' weighs over a ton and is the size of a small lorry it's prudent not to mess. I wondered what Kevin would do. What would I do in his place? The bull charged again but he must have hurt his head that time because he shook it from side to side and started to graze the grass.

'Serves you damn well right,' Kevin shouted at him.

Richard scrambled up the bank and squeezed through the hedge. He apologised profusely to Kevin and explained how Performer came to be in the field.

'If there's anything we can do to help you clear up after the fire you only have to say. You know that,' said Kevin seriously.

'How are you going to get him back?' shouted Desmond over the top of the hedge.

Richard was about to answer when I chipped in.

'If that was a ram I would show him some ewes and he would be sure to follow them,' I suggested.

'That's a good idea John,' Richard agreed from the other field.

We left Richard with Performer and the rest of us went back to the farm. There Desmond led the way to a cow in a loose box; she had calved the morning before. She was a quiet, gentle old girl and we drove her slowly down the fields. Performer was then driven back to the hedge. He spotted the cow but couldn't get back through the hedge so we walked the cow along one side of the hedge and him on the other until we came to a gap, he then jumped down into the ditch again and came up the other side and into the field. He looked a sight and no mistake, legs caked in mud and bits of hedge sticking out all over the place. Even the cow was taken aback at the sight of him. We drove the cow in front and he followed placidly behind back to the farm, we drove her into the bullpen, he followed and then we got her out again.

'I've had enough of farming to last me for years,' Richard sighed. 'Why didn't I take up something less exciting – like being a stuntman' he added.

I think we'd all had our fill of farming for the time being. Desmond set off for home, leaving the rest of us there. I could tell Richard was deeply upset.

'Look at it John, it's a disaster area. Bosworth field wouldn't have looked this bad in fourteen whatever it was.'

I could hear the desolation in his voice.

'When are you going to tell your father?' I asked.

'Ah well, now that is the six million dollar question isn't it? When am I going to tell him?' he shrugged.

'I'd tell him now if I were you,' said Elizabeth who had just joined us.

'Oh Liz, give it a rest. I can't tell him yet, I've got to psyche myself up for that.'

'Well better sooner than later. Do it now, Richard. The longer you leave it the worse it will be.'

I tacitly agreed with her.

Richard took the bull by the horns, so to speak, and shuffled off into the house grumbling 'nagging women' and 'glad I'm not married'. After a while he returned and we were amazed to see him looking quite pleased with himself, he actually had a smile on his face. He said he had just spoken with his father on the telephone and told him there had been a small fire at the farm, but it was nothing to worry about and there was just a bit of cleaning up to do. It was the words 'small fire' and 'bit of cleaning up' that made me wince. His father was worried at first and started to panic. He wanted to come home straight away but Richard pacified him and assured him it was only a 'small' fire so he agreed to stay. Richard certainly looked a lot more cheerful and relaxed now that he had got it off his chest. He had looked ghastly but now it was as if a great weight had been lifted off his shoulders.

I left the farm then, I had work to do at the school. Although it was Saturday and the school was closed I had to make sure the livestock were settled and there were other jobs to attend to. Jane would have fed the animals for me but she would have left by now. Jane was one of my rural studies senior pupils, very reliable. My three helpers went back to their campsite to try and salvage what was left of their short break. Richard was going to cart all the burnt straw and ashes to a corner of the field out of sight from the rest of the farm.

'What the eye doesn't see, eh John?' he said with a cheeky wink.

It would take a few days of hard slog to get the farm as neat as it usually was. The barn was completely burnt out but some of the silage might be salvaged. I only hoped the farm was well insured.

At nine o'clock that evening Richard telephoned me – my heart sank, what on earth was the matter now?'

'My father just telephoned me John.'

'Oh yes.'

'Oh yes. He wasn't very happy, gave me a right ear bending. He had just called Desmond who, bless his heart, sang like a canary and spilled the whole can of beans. Dad said, "The Dutch barn has gone, about 700 round bales were burnt, a thousand conventional bales were burnt, cattle nearly died and the place looks as if a bomb hit it and you call that a small fire?" Well, the rest of it, John, was unrepeatable.'

'Yes, I can well imagine.'

'He had thrown all his clothes into a suitcase, but mother managed to get there in time and made him unpack again. I agreed with her, there's nothing he can do that Desmond and I can't manage, you know, cleaning up and such, anyway he's agreed to stay. I tell you John I couldn't be doing with him on my back just now.'

'I'm glad he's decided to stay,' I said soothingly.

'Yes, you and me, both. If he saw this place he'd have a dickey fit.'

I nodded in agreement although he couldn't see me.

'One thing's for sure I've got to get this place looking immaculate again before he gets back or my life won't be worth living. Thank the Lord I've got five whole days to do it in. I'll get it done even if I have to work twenty-five hours a day.

'You'll do it Richard,' I said confidently.

'Do you think we'll laugh about this one day John?' he asked.

'Mmm,' I replied thoughtfully, 'not for a long time Richard, a very long time. That was a night to remember.'

For the next five days, and evenings, Richard beavered away cleaning up the mess. By the time Mr and Mrs Jonas arrived back from holiday all the debris had been cleared away. All that was left for Mr Jonas to do was sort out the insurance. Everything must have been done to his satisfaction as he and Mrs Jonas went away again four months later.

To Jersey? I don't know but I told Richard his father would get a taste for the good life.

Chapter Two
The Case Of The Missing Bicycle

The fire was of course a very horrible and nasty experience for the Jonas family, but life went on, both for the Jonases and for the students at my school. After the fire things were comparatively quiet until the following spring when lambing was in full force. This can bring its own problems and crises but these paled into insignificance compared to some of the students' problems.

School was over for the day and everyone was heading for home, all except one boy who was heading for me like an Intercity 125.

'Sir, sir,' he called. 'My bike's gone.'

He was in the first throes of panic with a bright red face and fighting for breath. 'Simon, calm down. Now what do you mean it's gone? Has it vanished into thin air, disappeared off the face of the Earth? Maybe it's been hijacked in a space ship by marauding aliens?' I said in a somewhat sarcastic voice.

Choosing to ignore my caustic comments he carried on.

'No, sir. You don't understand. It's been nicked – sorry, sir, stolen' he gasped.

I looked dubiously at him. He was certainly very distressed and appeared ready to explode at any given moment.

'Now quieten down a bit and let's be rational about this. Where did you last see it?' I asked, trying to instil a bit of common sense into the situation.

'Where I left it.'

This wasn't quite the response I wanted but I persevered.

'And where was that?'

'In the bike sheds at ten to nine this morning.'

Now we were getting somewhere.

'I see, and did you lock it?' I asked.

He replied emphatically. 'Yes, sir. Definitely. Absolutely.

Rabbits On Report

Positively. It's a combination lock and I'm the only one that knows what the combination is.'

'Have you looked at the back of the sheds or along the edge of the school drive?' I asked.

'Sir' he sighed. 'I've looked everywhere. It's ten past four now, I've been searching for twenty-five minutes.'

I could sense the desperation creeping in.

'Come on I'll help you look,' I said.

Simon led the way to the sheds. I could tell he was getting in a state, the tragic look on his face was pitiable.

'My heart's thumping and my stomach's doing back flips,' he confided.

'Well don't worry unduly yet. I'm sure it will turn up.' I tried to console him.

'I wish I could be as sure,' he said disconsolately.

The Case Of The Missing Bicycle

'Someone could be playing a joke on you.'

'If they are, it's not a very funny one,' he said.

I felt so sorry for him. He wasn't the brightest bulb in the box but he was a trier and a good trier always gets full marks from me. He was a good worker and a member of my form – form 11S1. At the time of the bicycle incident he was fifteen. I wanted to help him but deep down, as the minutes ticked away and there was no sign of the machine, I began to fear the worst.

Perhaps Simon was right and his bicycle had been stolen. This put a sinister aspect to it. If the cycle had been stolen it meant someone, unauthorised and unsupervised, had been on school property.

We half ran across the playground as a strong wind blew hard in our faces. We then walked through the school corridor and out at the front of the school to the bike sheds.

The bike sheds were low wooden sheds, open fronted with all the bikes stored in one row. It was empty now except for three bikes, which probably belonged to members of the football team who were playing a team at another school.

'I always leave my bike parked here,' said Simon indicating an empty space.

'Do you always leave it there?' I asked. 'I keep looking at these three left here, obviously none of these belong to you.'

'No, sir, my bike is far better than these.' He turned his nose up derisively.

'What make and colour is it?' I asked.

'It's a Raleigh racing bike and it's blue. It was my main Christmas present off my mum and dad. It's only four months old.'

We looked at the back of the bicycle sheds first. This was a favourite haunt of the young Romeos and Juliets of the day and the crafty fag brigade but there was nothing there. Then we tried the rear of the science labs but all to no avail as there was no sign of the bicycle. We then checked all around the edge of the school buildings, the school drive, the flowerbeds, behind trees and hedges before ending up in the rural studies department.

About seven pupils were carrying out the task of feeding the animals. Maybe one of these pupils had ridden his bicycle and had hidden it, or at least one of them might have seen it and knew its whereabouts. We asked everyone if they had seen it. No one had. We checked the area again ourselves, there was nothing so we returned to the bicycle sheds in the vain hope that it had somehow magically appeared.

'Let's try the school playing field,' I suggested.

Simon agreed but I could see by the look on his face that he knew it was useless.

It took ten minutes to search the playing field and as we retraced our steps Simon said, 'What do we do now, sir? My dad will go mad.'

'Do you want to telephone him?' I asked.

'Not really, sir.' Simon shook his head. 'Anyway, both mum and dad are at work.'

'Well Simon, it certainly looks like a theft and needs to be reported to the police.'

'Yes, sir.'

'We must inform the headmaster first then we can ring from the office.'

I knocked on the headmaster's door but there was no reply. I would have to deal with it all. I headed towards the secretary's office – Simon followed looking glummer than ever.

'Cheer up,' I said. 'The police might find it.'

'Yes, and pigs might fly,' he replied.

Mrs Lumsden, the school secretary, was busy at her computer.

'This lad has had his bicycle stolen and I need to inform the police. May I use your telephone please?'

'Oh be my guest, Mr Terry. It will make a change to hear a call going out instead of coming in, the wretched thing hasn't stopped ringing all day.'

I spoke to a lady on the police switchboard and she told me an officer would be along to see us shortly.

The Case Of The Missing Bicycle

I told her to tell the officer to meet us at the rural studies department. We then made a mad dash back to our school farm to make sure the others were feeding and looking after the livestock even though I wasn't standing over them.

All was going well – except for a rabbit, which had escaped from its hutch and was roaming around the lawn and being chased by two very excited pupils.

'Tell that rabbit if it doesn't get back in its hutch right now he's on report,' I cried as we ran past. The rabbit capitulated and was back in his hutch in no time at all.

Earlier in the day we had borrowed an old Ford tractor from Matt Corbutt, one of our farming neighbours. It was hitched to our farm trailer. Three pupils were busy cleaning out the brick building that housed our show rams and ewes; they were forking out the manure into wheelbarrows then unloading these onto our trailer. The work was going well.

About a quarter of an hour had elapsed when a police officer arrived in a new Metro. I introduced myself and then Simon.

'So you're the young man with the missing bicycle are you?'

'Stolen actually, sir,' Simon persisted.

'All right, tell me about it,' said the officer in a firm but kindly voice.

'I locked my Raleigh racing bike in the school shed at ten to nine this morning. I've been in school all day and when I went to collect it to ride it home it was gone.'

'Right. Can you give me a better description of it, better still, can you give me the serial number?'

'Yes I can,' said Simon proudly. 'It's dark blue with drop racing handles. Just a minute I've got the serial number in my diary.' He took the diary out of his trouser pocket and flicked through the pages until he came to the one he wanted.

'Here it is,' he said triumphantly. He read the number out while the policeman wrote it down.

'Can you just repeat that for me please lad. Make sure

I've got it down right.'

Simon read the number again, slowly and clearly.

The officer looked at him.

'Well I must admit I am most impressed, ten out of ten for that. We take dozens of statements with regard to stolen bicycles and you are the first person who has been able to give the number. Good lad.'

Simon looked really pleased with himself and I was very impressed with him too. He had handled the situation well.

'It was my dad's suggestion that I put the number in my diary,' admitted Simon.

'I'll tell you now Simon, we've had a spate of thefts in this area. A gang of two or three men have got a small van and we are sure they are responsible for a number of crimes. Stealing to order. At one school, only a fortnight ago, five bicycles were stolen.'

'It looks as if mine has gone the same way.'

'It could be, but I can't understand why they didn't take more than one bike and why take one that was locked? I bet some of the bikes in the shed weren't locked up.'

I could see a faint glimmer of hope in Simon's eyes.

'Have you got the registration number of the van?' he asked.

'No such luck, son. We think it is a Ford Escort – white or cream in colour, but that's all we've got to go on.

The officer was ready to leave and as he got into his car he said he would inform us of any developments.

'Is it insured?' I asked Simon.

'Not as an individual item but it might be on the house insurance,' he replied. 'I'll have to check when I get home.'

We left the bicycle sheds and went back to the school farm. I offered to drive him home as he lived four miles away. I was also thinking that perhaps his parents wouldn't be so hard on him if I was present. He'd had enough of a hard time for one day.

'My mum and dad will be home from work now, sir. I know my dad, he'll go mental.'

'You mean he'll be very angry,' I corrected him.

'Angry, mental, ballistic, you name it, that will be him, sir.

The Case Of The Missing Bicycle

He might not even believe I locked it but I did, sir, I honestly did.'

Pupils working on the school farm had finished their tasks and had changed out of working clothes into school uniform. Simon and myself walked around the buildings checking that all the stock had been fed and watered and made comfortable for the night.

The work done we got into my car and I drove Simon home. For the entire journey the only time he spoke was to give me directions.

We eventually arrived at a large four-bedroomed detached house, in a very upmarket area. I parked on the tarmac drive behind his father's new Mercedes. Simon led the way to the door.

'Oh well, here goes, time to face the music,' he said, bracing himself for the imminent storm. 'You will come in with me sir, won't you? It might help to soften the blow.'

'Yes, I'll come in with you,' I agreed.

His mother opened the door before we reached the step.

'What's he done?' she demanded. 'Is he in trouble?'

Before I could say anything Simon answered.

'No mum. Not real trouble.'

'And what's that supposed to mean?' she said.

Then father appeared.

'What's he been up to then?' he asked.

'Dad it's my bike. It's been stolen,' Simon blurted out the bad news, eager to get it over with.

'Don't shout then. I'm in front of you not in the next street. Calm down for goodness sake,' his father replied. 'Hello Mr Terry. What's he on about?'

I had met Simon's mother and father at parents' evenings.

'I'm afraid Simon has had his bicycle stolen from school,' I replied.

His father looked at Simon and shook his head in disbelief. He didn't speak for what seemed like hours. I thought he was biting back his anger for my benefit. Then he said, 'Oh Simon, what are we going to do with you? You didn't go to school on your bicycle this morning. It was raining cats and dogs so I took you in the car. Don't you remember?'

Case closed.

Chapter Three
A Cast Of Hundreds

One day I received a telephone call from the BBC who wanted to do a television programme about a school farm. Two days after the telephone call two gentlemen from the BBC's farming programme arrived at the school to study the possibilities of a ten-minute film which would hopefully go out to one and a half million viewers on Easter Sunday.

That was a pleasant surprise. Matt Large was the producer and Len Cotterill was the presenter – I had watched Len on screen many times, usually while eating my Sunday roast.

They arrived at break time and asked to sit in on my next lesson – a discourse on goat keeping to a fifth-year class of twenty-six pupils. It was apparent that this was a 'dummy run'. Whether we were to be accepted for the national programme would depend on my afternoon's performance and the behaviour of my pupils during the lesson.

The two sat at the back of the classroom while I launched into a fifteen-minute talk. I invited questions from the pupils, for whom this was a new topic, and showed pictures of the main breeds.

I noticed that as well as the pupils the BBC staff were also taking notes and I wondered whether they were finding fault with my teaching methods or working out lighting and camera angles. From the way they were waving their arms about I surmised it must be the latter.

I had some difficulty in concentrating on the lesson – I was becoming star struck before filming had even started.

For the last ten minutes of the lesson we all went outside to inspect our goats and discuss their housing and feeding. My pupils were behaving exceptionally well but regarding the visitors with some suspicion.

As for me, it was rather like being on teaching practice again and I expected I would be in for the usual critical appraisal.

Nothing of the sort happened. When the class had been dismissed Matt and Len both enthused with complimentary expressions like 'great' and splendid'.

'Can you repeat that lesson for us next week?' asked Matt.

'Yes. I'd be delighted,' I replied.

'It's just what we need,' he said.

I had just had the film rehearsal without knowing it.

That wasn't the end of it. School had officially finished for the day but pupils of all ages were coming with offers of help with the livestock.

'Can we stay and watch?' asked Matt.

'Of course, even though I do say it myself my pupils are very well organised at looking after the livestock both before and after school.'

Matthew began to feed the ewes and lambs in their individual pens and Heather fed and watered the rabbits. Elaine and Gail milked the goats and Catherine cleaned out and fed the pigs while Vanessa fed and watered the calves. They made a great team and made a special effort to impress Matt and Len.

Matt said they would definitely come out to make the film, starting next Monday and working until Tuesday evening – two full days.

At 9.15am on the Monday morning they all duly arrived, three car loads of them. I was introduced to a cameraman, a lighting man, a sound engineer, an electrician (known to all and sundry as 'Sparks', what else) and a producer's assistant, the only lady on the team. Including Matt and Len it added up to seven. It was surely costing a fortune.

It was a delight to watch the expressions on the faces of my third-year pupils when they arrived for their lesson and found batteries of lights, all switched on, and a camera all ready to shoot. They were my best third-year group, always well behaved and I was confident they wouldn't let me down. But I still explained that they must be on their best behaviour as this was the BBC and some of them would be film stars.

They took out their exercise books and assumed they would be finishing their work on plant propagation. My students were still looking around and not really concentrating when I said, 'We are going to leave plant propagation today, due to our visitors wanting to film some of our livestock.'

'Which livestock?' asked Gemma.

'Goats,' I replied.

Some of my students even began to comb their hair. The atmosphere was electric when the clapperboard was produced for 'slate one – take one'. It was the first time I had seen a clapperboard, or a production assistant taking notes and I came to realise what a professional job this was going to be.

I was filmed in close-up, talking and asking questions. Then the lights were moved and the cameraman focused on the pupils as they answered me and took notes. At the end of the lesson they were reluctant to go on to 'boring' history and engaged the incoming class – another third-year group – in an animated exchange on their acting debut.

The new group followed the film crew to a couple of trees on the lawn where two girls were positioned with our two in-kid goats and – at a signal from Matt – the girls led the goats forward towards us.

Then the fun started. One goat, Anna, decided she didn't like so many people about and dug her heels in. Her attendant, Julia, pulled and pushed until she was red in the face and in danger of bursting a blood vessel but Anna wouldn't budge. The other goat, Penny was led in front of her but after three steps decided it wasn't her job to lead the parade and she stopped. We had a strike on. Soon we had half-a-dozen pupils pulling and pushing two extremely stubborn goats.

'Cut,' Matt shouted. 'What do they want? An Equity card? It's always the same with animals and children,' he added wryly. He didn't have to tell me. I knew working with animals and children is a dangerous combination. I knew from experience, I worked with the little beggars every day, rain or shine, Sundays and Bank holidays included and some of the scrapes they landed us in wouldn't stand up to close scrutiny.

By now everyone, with the exception of Matt and myself, was rolling about the lawn with ill-concealed glee.

'Can we try the donkey-and-carrot trick?' Matt pleaded.

One of the girls rattled a bucket of nuts in front of the goats and greed overcame their inhibitions: they walked towards us performing perfectly. No need to call in ACAS.

'That was excellent. Why didn't we do that in the first place?' Matt said.

Next they filmed me talking about the goats and the points to look for when buying a goat. I emphasised that we were monitoring Anna closely as she was due to kid that day.

At lunch time I realised that I had forgotten to observe the rule of every teaching day – to check the staff notice board before lessons start, to find out if you've lost any free periods or are needed to cover for an absent teacher. I knew I hadn't any 'frees' so Mr Beech couldn't tell me off about that. Nevertheless, there could be something important.

'Here he is, our answer to John Wayne,' observed Mr Petty as I entered the staff room.

'John Wayne's dead,' pointed out the headmaster.

'The hell I am.' I treated them to my version of Big John.

Miss Perrin, the home economics teacher, decided to put her ten pennyworth in. 'Oh look at you. What time have you got to be back in Burton's window then? You are looking smart today John. Not a hair out of place, nice jacket and trousers, no sheep muck on your shoes, what's the occasion? Are you getting married?'

'He's making a full-length feature film. Haven't you heard? Metro-Goldwyn-Mayer, no less. He's the one that bangs the gong at the beginning,' said Mr Petty.

It was all good-humoured banter but I couldn't stay and join in. I ran back to the department.

'We're all ready for lunch,' said Jack the cameraman. 'Can you show me a public house?'

'You're talking to him,' chipped in a voice from just behind my elbow. I turned to find one of my pupils who, unnoticed, had managed to get himself in on the act.

For some unaccountable reason my lot had got me down as a dedicated drinker, which I am not. Just because I enjoyed a pint or two at the weekend with like-minded friends i.e. farmers, according to the children I was the world's greatest party animal.

'How long have you been there and what do you want?' I asked rather sharply.

'Ten minutes and I've got a message for you,' came the equally sharp reply.

'What is it?'

'What?'

'The message.'

'Oh, that.'

'Yes, that.' His eyes were everywhere, taking in the lights and cameras.

'I'm going for my dinner.'

'Fine. Go on then.' It was clear the lad was star struck and wanted to be on film. Jack was highly amused by the incident.

'I think I'd better rephrase that,' he said through the tears.

'Yes I think you had,' I said, trying to control my own mirth and failing dismally.

'Right. Can you point us in the direction of a public house, inn or hostelry?' he asked.

'Indeed I can,' I replied. 'There's one almost on the doorstep.'

'Come with us and have a meal,' Matt suggested.

'Oh what a great idea.' I never went out for lunch – in fact on many days I didn't even get a school dinner. I realised then that I was famished.

Although it wasn't very far they insisted on going in their cars and I led the way in mine. Matt bought the drinks (soft ones) and they all thought it hilarious when I ordered shepherds pie off the menu for my lunch. While waiting for it I talked farming with Matt, constantly looking at my watch.

'Are you on a time and motion study?' Len asked. 'What's the rush?'

'The afternoon session starts at twenty-five past one and it's ten past already,' I answered. 'I'm going to have a job to eat my lunch before registration.'

When the food finally arrived it was twenty-two minutes past. I had three minutes to eat my pie, which was piping hot, and get back on duty.

'I'll take this with me,' I told the waitress.

'Oh no you can't. We don't do take aways,' she protested.

'Look, I'll return the plate and cutlery later this afternoon,' I promised. I said cheerio to the film crew and picked my way through the crowded bar with my plate of hot shepherds pie, potatoes, peas, carrots and gravy held aloft.

The steaming hot dinner sat on the passenger seat of my car tempting my nostrils and taste buds all the way back to school. Needless to say I drove very carefully. I didn't want to spill a precious drop. Thankfully there were no traffic-calming humps to negotiate.

My form sat waiting for the roll call to begin and gazed in astonishment as I sashayed in carrying my plate. I sat and ate some of it after marking the register and I was still eating it when my fifth years arrived for their lesson.

'What have you got there, sir?' asked Paul.

'Shepherds pie,' I replied.

'Oh,' he paused, then said, 'My mum made a cottage pie once.'

'So?'

'The council condemned it.'

This was the cue for the whole class to erupt.

Sir had done it again. They had set me up and I had walked right into it. Just when you think you have the measure of them some smart Alec proves you wrong.

Between mouthfuls I told them to simmer down and finish off their notes from last week.

After a while, Paul popped out to check on the livestock. I had just finished my dinner when he raced back into the classroom in a high state of excitement.

'Sir, I think Penny is about to kid,' he shouted. I chased out after him, followed by half-a-dozen pupils.

We watched her for five minutes and saw that his diagnosis was correct.

'It would be great to get the birth on film,' I said. 'But the crew are having their lunch at the pub. I could go and get them but if Mr Beech found out that I'd left the premises there would be serious trouble.'

'You can't go anyway,' said practical Paul. 'You've got to stay with Penny.'

'I'll go,' volunteered David.

'I'll come with you,' said Pam 'I could just do with a Bacardi and coke.'

'Don't even think about it. You're far too young and what if the headmaster found out?' I said decisively. 'David, you go, you're the biggest and the oldest and, I hope, the most sensible.'

'How will I recognise them, sir?'

'You'll find a group of six men and one lady, on the far side of the lounge sitting underneath the long window.'

'No problem, sir. I always get served when I go out with my friends.'

I saw no reason to doubt him.

'Here, take this back for me please.' I handed him my plate, knife and fork.

I returned to the classroom. I didn't want to leave Penny on her own, and I couldn't leave my class on their own – I was about to panic. I did a quick head count and it came as no surprise to find that in addition to David five lads and two girls were conspicuous by their absence.

'Where are they? Has the headmaster sent for them?' I asked with sinking heart, knowing only too well where they were.

'No, sir. They've gone to the pub with David,' said Pam, confirming my worst suspicions.

I ran outside but it was too late, all I could do was hope they would stay outside and leave it to David to go in. I then called my class outside and we went to keep a watch on Penny.

Seconds later the film crew arrived back at the classroom. Surely the pupils hadn't been that quick.

'Have you seen any of my pupils?' I asked.

'No,' replied Matt.

'You must have, I sent them to tell you that Penny the goat is about to kid any minute now.'

'We certainly haven't seen them,' said Len. The crew began to set up their lights in the goat pen and at that point Mr Beech arrived, petrifying me with his uncanny sense of timing. His timing was impeccable. If everything is going to plan Murphy's law says something will go wrong and sure enough it does. In our case if a crisis appeared so did the headmaster. He gave me palpitations because if you've got a petulant pig or a truculent turkey hell bent on destroying your career as a rural studies teacher you are truly in the lap of the gods. Cold sweats? I know all about those, I've had a few in my time. It wasn't just our department, every teacher at the school at some time went weak at the knees; it was just that ours was the main trauma department.

'We're all very excited,' I said. 'One of the goats is about to kid.'

'Oh. Ah. Very well Mr Terry. I'll just leave you to it.'

Although he would never admit it in a hundred years, Mr Beech didn't like the gory bits. He began to walk across the playground and I heaved a sigh of relief until, to my horror, he turned and went into my classroom.

'Oh no,' I groaned. I ran after him, my heart in jive rhythm. But he was telling the class about a trip to the theatre he was organising and once again I experienced a sense of relief, although it was short lived. The headmaster turned to me and said: 'So, Mr Terry, it appears a lot of your pupils are absent today.'

'Oh no, no,' I jabbered. 'They're just doing an outdoor practical job,' I said, bending the truth to breaking point.

'Ah,' he said, giving me a dubious look. I don't think he believed me for one minute. However he gave me the benefit of the doubt and then left. In true Whitehall farce fashion in walked the missing pupils, puffing and wheezing like old traction engines.

David was the spokesman. 'Sir' he gulped for air. 'Sir, we took the short cut to save time. We got to the pub and we all burst in – just like in a western film it was, sir.'

I began to feel a little peculiar. What was coming next?

'Julian shouted "the goat's kidding" but no one was sitting where you said, sir, and it all went quiet. Everyone looked at us as if we were mad, the staff came in from all over the place and the manager called us a bunch of hooligans and shouted at us to clear out, sir.'

David put on his hard-done by look.

'When I got back to the playground I realised I still had your plate, knife and fork in my hand so I had to run back to the pub again, sir, and tell them you sent it. Do you know what the manager said, sir?'

'I can't even begin to guess but I'm sure you're going to tell me.'

'He said "Oh no, not him again."'

The afternoon wore on and Penny seemed to be making little progress with her kidding. The crew decided to leave the lights set up in the pen and press on with their original schedule, which was to film the class planting some early potatoes. I had bought the seed potatoes from a local garden centre at the weekend – when I told them they would be used for a BBC film they gave me ten percent off and the owner said he would be watching out – for the potatoes not me.

The sun was shining and conditions were ideal for outdoor filming. After the planting session a third-year class were issued with forks and spades and put fertiliser around the trees.

Matt discussed the next day's shooting with me and the crew packed up and went home – all except Matt who had booked in at a local hotel. Three minutes after their cars had left the school Penny revealed her water bag and a little while later two handsome twins came into the world, a billy and a nanny. It seemed as if she had deliberately waited until the film crew had gone and she gave a cheeky look as if to say 'I did that on purpose.'

I was so delighted by the twins' arrival I didn't mind missing my tea. There was no time for eating as I was due to make a radio recording at BBC Northampton at 6.30pm. I arrived at the studio to find it all locked up. A disc jockey was working away in there but all my lunatic waving and shouting at the window failed to attract his attention.

Eventually a cleaning lady let me in.

'You frightened the life out of me, banging and yelling like that,' she said.

'I'm really sorry about that but I've an appointment with Tony at 6.30pm and I'm late already.'

'Come and sit down while I tell him you're here. Would you like a cup of coffee?' She was obviously used to soothing harassed broadcasters.

'Oh would I!' I said.

Within twenty minutes my interview was taped and I was on my way back to school to start my nightly routine of 'stock taking'. I hoped for a reasonable night's sleep, but when I checked the ewes at three in the morning I had to help one of them, Alison, to produce a single ewe lamb. I knew that Matt would be disappointed. He desperately wanted to get a birth on film.

Tuesday morning was dark and dismal but it brought a very pleasant surprise. Matt asked if the crew could stay an extra two days – until Thursday evening. Instead of using our story for part of the programme they wanted to devote the whole programme to us. Naturally, I was overjoyed.

Mr Bell the deputy headmaster, was covering my lessons at the start of the day in order to enable Matt to do an in-depth interview with me but this idea was shelved when the monthly supply of feedstuff was delivered. The cameras were moved outside and I borrowed some pupils from Mrs Charles's RE lesson to be filmed unloading the lorry.

'We'll make you into a television star,' Matt joked with Bill, the driver.

'I'd have put my clean overalls on if I'd known,' Bill answered back 'and maybe a tie.'

When we finally got down to my interview my chat with Len about how I started the school farm was punctuated by several interruptions. The first was from a girl sent by Miss Perrin, the home economics teacher, to buy some eggs. Soon afterwards we had to stop again because the ducks had got out of their run and again five minutes later because Mr Searle wanted an urgent report to be written on a pupil who had 'gone off the rails'.

A more useful and welcome interruption came in the person of a former pupil, Derek Greenfield, who had been working on a farm in Norway and was spending a few days in Britain before moving to a farming job in America. Matt told him not to go too far as he would like to interview him.

During my interview Len remarked on how tidy the school farm looked and on the absence of graffiti.

'We do get graffiti occasionally' I said 'but when I find the culprit he's made to clean it off after school.'

Had anyone written anything about me?

'Yes, once. In big letters on that back desk there, someone had written 'Terry likes his raddle' At first I was disgusted but then it occurred to me how many schoolchildren know what a raddle is?'

This cause great amusement among the crew until Matt said, 'It's all very well us laughing but not everyone knows what a raddle is. For the benefit of our non-farming viewers would you be good enough to explain what one is.'

'Certainly,' I replied. 'It's a harness the ram wears. A crayon fits into it and when the ram serves a ewe the colour rubs off on to the ewe's back. That's how we know which ewes have been served.'

After my interview it was Derek Greenfield's turn.

'I didn't expect this, Mr Terry,' he said, fussing with his hair and tie.

Derek said some very complimentary things about the school and emphasised that it was the rural studies department that had aroused his interest in farming. While the lights were set up in the classroom our prize certificates and rosettes were filmed to be spliced into a sequence showing our ram being prepared for the show ring.

Then the lights and camera were transferred to that holy of holies, the headmaster's study. It was a surprise move as far as I was concerned and I didn't want to miss it. Mr Beech, on the other hand, had different ideas. When he saw me he glared and put his foot down. 'That will be all from you Mr Terry. You can leave this to me thank you,' he snorted.

How I wished I could have been a fly on the wall at that interview but the door was closed against me, I would have to wait for the broadcast. I wondered if he would tell them about our little disagreements over the years and how he wished he was headmaster of a 'normal' school.

'What did Mr Beech say?' I asked Matt as nonchalantly as I could. They were just going to the pub for lunch.

'Oh wouldn't you like to know,' Matt grinned. 'That's confidential. You'll just have to wait and see.'

After lunch they filmed me carding and trimming a ram ready for showing. I told a group of fourth-year spectators how some exhibitors cheat by using hair dyes on their sheep. When school finished, the lights were set up in our large wooden building.

The crew had almost finished an interview with Matthew about our flock of sheep when I noticed that another of our goats – Anna – was close to kidding and even as I watched her water bag was out.

'The goat's going to kid,' I cried excitedly. 'Stop filming Matthew, forget him and bring the lights down here, don't just stand there – move!

My teacher's authority was asserting itself in my panicky desire for action.

'Put that light over there at this angle, come on, mind the cable, get on with it.'

Our biology teacher, Mr Appleton, was watching this scene and he was almost doubled up at my harsh tirade. He caught hold of my sleeve and pulled me to one side.

'John,' he said through his laughter. 'What do you think you're doing? Are you the director and producer now?'

I realised then that in the space of a few minutes I had done what it had taken Matt years of training to achieve. I had taken over the entire outside broadcast crew of the BBC.

Mercifully the crew were tolerant of my antics. Quickly they set up their equipment in time to capture the appearance of two front legs. Anna strained, I pulled gently. It was a big, strong and healthy billy kid and the whole process was on film as well as being witnessed by an interested audience of youngsters and accompanied by a chorus of 'Aah. Look. Isn't he sweet' and Anna got a round of applause.

Len asked me, on camera, if I thought it was a good thing for the pupils to watch. Yes indeed, I told him. Birth is the most natural process in the world, it was the modern trend for husbands to be present as their wives gave birth and hopefully, when our lads became fathers they would think nothing of it.

The kid was soon taking nourishment from his mother. What a perfect ending to a day's filming.

That night Matt asked me to telephone a local farmer so he could film the purchase of some calves. I called Dennis, our usual calf supplier, to see if he had a couple of Hereford x Friesians to sell.

'Yes John, as a matter of fact I've got two very good strong bull calves. When are you coming to look at them?'

'Ten o'clock tomorrow morning. There's just one small point.'

'Oh yes?' he said suspiciously 'and what might that be?'

'I'll be bringing along a film crew of seven from the BBC.'

'You'd better bloody not,' he said.

'Oh come on Dennis. Where's your sense of adventure?'

'I haven't got one.'

'Please,' I pleaded. 'Everyone will be so disappointed if you can't do it.'

'W-e-l-l …'

He's weakening, I thought, definitely weakening.

'Dennis? Go on, take a chance.'

'Ooh! The things I do for you,' he said. 'Just remember, you owe me.'

'Dennis, you're a star,' I said.

Wednesday morning dawned bright and beautiful. I was up early to clean the car and trailer. Mr Bell, the deputy headmaster, again covered my lessons to give me the morning free.

I left a message with the school secretary.

'If anyone telephones for me, tell them I'm out on location with the BBC.'

It sounded very grand.

Matt wanted to film me actually driving, like in a cops and robbers movie.

Jack, the cameraman squatted in the passenger seat. John the lighting man placed a light with a blue plastic cover near the gear stick. Clive the soundman sat in the back with Matt. A microphone was pinned on me.

As I drove I explained that we were off to buy calves from Dennis Golby, a farmer who was noted as a 'hard' business man, and that I would try very hard to knock his price down.

At the farm we were greeted by Julia, his wife.

'I'm not sure if Dennis will be all right,' she said.

'Why? What's happened?'

'Well, he's been suffering from nerves ever since you rang and he's polished off the best part of a bottle of Scotch in the last hour.'

Dennis walked, or rather, wobbled up to us. His face was redder than usual.

'I've had a drink or two to settle my nerves,' he slurred.

'One or two? More like six or seven,' declared Julia.

I was filmed backing the trailer up to the calf building, shaking hands with Dennis and getting down to business.

'These are two lovely calves John,' Dennis said, opening the door so that we could see them.

'Bull calves aren't they?' I asked. 'They certainly are good ones. How much do you want for them? Before you name your price I must tell you that school funds are very low. I'm farming on a shoestring budget, but I also understand you have a business to run so what do you think they're worth?'

'Well I took some fellow ones to market last week and they made £145 apiece.'

'Really? I thought they would be worth £120 apiece.'

'No, no John, I couldn't let them go at that price. They're three weeks old.'

'How about if I went to £125 then?'

'You're not giving much are you? Look, seeing as how I haven't got to take them to market and pay the auctioneer's commission I'll let you have them for £130 – each.'

'That sounds reasonable enough,' I said. 'But would you be prepared to throw in half a bag of substitute calf milk?'

'Would you like the bloody shed as well?

Did I detect a hint of sarcasm?

'Come on – half a bag.'

'Oh all right then, you win again, I can do that for you,' Dennis said with a forced smile.

'You're a tough cookie John,' said Matt. 'The viewers will love it, especially that last bit.' The crew was thoroughly enjoying the performance.

We were having coffee in Dennis's enormous farmhouse when suddenly a terrific bang from outside sent us all scurrying to the window. Peering out we saw that a lorry had left the road, crashed through the farm fence and struck a moving tractor, which had been turned on its side. The drivers had escaped with cuts and bruises but the air was blue. Dennis telephoned for the ambulance and the police.

Most of us were in the kitchen when the police patrolman came in and there was great hilarity when, instead of asking what had happened, he opened with 'Oh, it's John Terry.'

Everyone immediately jumped to the conclusion that I had a criminal record. In fact, I was teaching Hillary, the policeman's daughter, and had met him at parents' evenings.

When the ambulance arrived to take the injured to hospital Dennis decided he'd had enough excitement for one day and would we all please leave as he had a splitting headache.

'I'm not surprised,' said Julia unsympathetically. 'He's hung over, that's what's wrong with him. He's just about bought shares in the distillery.'

After lunch filming went on with work in the greenhouse – planting seeds and watering – and moving of a group of ewes and lambs into a paddock. It continued after school had ended. A team of my young workers were filmed as they walked across the playground with brooms, buckets and barrows, then each was interviewed talking about the animals they were looking after.

On the final day of the shooting a Billy Bunter lookalike, thirteen years old Donald, was immortalised in the act of reading funny bits from 'Pigs In The Playground' while munching a mountain of crisps and chocolate supplied free by the BBC. Donald thought all his birthdays had come at once. He couldn't believe his luck.

There was a final interview with me, in which I revealed my ultimate ambition – to win the championship prize for the best sheep at the Royal Show.

Then it was time for the grand finale with a 'Ben Hur' style cast of 200 students showing my dream coming true.

Firstly I was given a hearty handshake. The championship rosette was placed on our ram, William. Dressed in my white coat I led him across the playground to be surrounded by an army of pupils all waving and cheering like mad.

Cameras on the roof recorded this scene of noisy jubilation. It was a rapturous ending for the film.

Matt told me they had used twenty-two cans of film – almost enough for a full-length feature film. Our completed film would last less than half an hour.

'I've spent far too much bloody money on this as it is,' he muttered, but I could see he was pleased with the operation.

I handed Jack my favourite single lens reflex camera so he could take some souvenir stills of a big group comprising the rest of the crew, the pupils and myself.

Matt seemed somewhat amused.

'You've asked the wrong one there, Jack will never get to grips with that – he can't even work a Box Brownie,' he roared. He was dead right, when the film was developed the pictures were awful. Heads cut off, feet missing, everybody leaning to starboard. Lord Lichfield didn't need to worry.

I was confident Jack's 'real' pictures would be infinitely better but the long wait for Easter Sunday and our programme was nevertheless a nerve-racking time.

Lots of scenes had been cut due to the time restriction but everyone I knew said how much they had enjoyed it and we received many letters from well wishers, viewers we didn't know and some we did.

I thought it was absolutely wonderful, a well-deserved tribute to our school farm and all who worked on it. And a sight more interesting than 'Ben Hur' any day.

The interview that had taken place in the inner sanctum – Mr Beech's office – had been at the back of my mind since the recording had been done and I waited with trepidation but I need not have worried. Mr Beech had said many complimentary things about the school farm and, surprisingly enough, about me too. Sometimes we aggravated him to death but he wasn't such a bad chap.

I wondered if it might be a good time to ask him if we could have a new tractor.

Chapter Four
Milk Fever And Disaster

As in all professions teaching and farming have their highs and lows. One day you are riding the crest of the wave and a few days later the wave troughs and there you are in the doldrums.

The crest of one of our waves was the good news that Windsor Coronets Crystal VI, our pedigree Jersey cow, was again in calf. Crystal had been purchased from the Queen about seven years previously. She looked fit and well and the pupils were counting the days until her calving date.

Her due date came and went and so did the next day.

'It looks as if it will be a bull calf,' said John pessimistically.

'It's a bit too early to tell yet.' I tried to be optimistic but John knew that if a cow is late to give birth more often than not she has a bull calf.

She was actually five days late but calved quite easily after school one Friday evening in June, with an audience of about fifteen interested and excited pupils in attendance. John was the first to lift the newborn calf's hind leg, it was a bull calf and we were all so disappointed. Jersey bull calves are of little value commercially. It is only a very few that are reared and kept on as breeding bulls.

Jerseys are a real dairy breed originating from Jersey and bred to give rich milk. When reared for beef they do not produce enough meat and muscle compared with Friesians and when compared to real beef breeds such as Charolais or Limousin they are hopeless. It is a hard fact that many Jersey bull calves are slaughtered soon after birth because they are worth so little.

When you only have one cow in your herd and have waited for about 280–284 days for your calf it is sure to be a disappointment when a bull calf is produced. I could understand John's frustration. Crystal had produced only two heifer calves over the years – Natalie and Elizabeth. Natalie had been reared up and sold just before she calved to a community farm in Wales. Elizabeth was sold at twelve months old to a farm in Staffordshire and she was achieving very good milk records. We were proud of her.

Two days after calving John came running into the mobile classroom. It was 8.30am and we had just started to do the feeding.

'Sir, I've just let Crystal out on to the grass and she can't walk properly, she's swaying from side to side,' he said.

John turned to go out again and I quickly followed him. I didn't like what I was hearing. Crystal was standing in the gateway looking absolutely dreadful.

'Let's get her back inside,' I said.

The two of us walked around, walking gently behind her and coaxed her back through the gateway.

'I'm afraid Crystal is showing all the symptoms of milk fever,' I said.

'What's that?' they asked.

'It isn't a fever, it's a badly named complaint,' I explained.

'Oh, like ringworm? That's not a worm at all, sir, it's a fungus,' interrupted Susan, one of my more intelligent pupils.

'That's exactly it Susan, well done. I'll telephone the vet first, then I'll explain it to you.'

I ran off to the office and telephoned the vet.

'Trouble John?' asked another teacher who was present.

'Oh and how. It's Crystal, she's not well at all.'

'Ah bless her, what's wrong?'

'Milk fever, I think.'

'Oh dear, it sounds serious.'

'Yes it can be.' Just then the call was answered and I was talking to the receptionist. She took all the details and promised to get a vet out as soon as possible. The minute my call was finished I rushed back to my worried students.

'Is the vet coming, sir?' asked Susan.

'Yes but I'm not sure how long we'll have to wait although they say it should be within the hour.'

'What is milk fever?' asked Joe.

'Well as I said before, it isn't a fever, it's caused by lack of calcium in the bloodstream. It's a fairly common complaint in cows, usually found within three days of calving. The

Milk Fever And Disaster

main symptoms are, as John saw, swaying from side to side and falling over. They can go into a coma, sometimes they groan and in some cases, not all, can prove fatal.'

'Could we have prevented it?' asked Susan.

'Yes,' I replied. 'You should always make sure that there is plenty of calcium in the cattle feed – obviously in this case there wasn't enough.'

'So it's all our fault then?' said John desolately.

'It's not one person's fault. We weren't quite diligent enough in watching the feed. There's no need for anyone to feel guilty, more experienced cattlemen than you have been caught out by it.'

'I wish the vet would get here,' said Susan.

Half an hour later the vet arrived and I was relieved to see it was David, a clever, experienced vet who had been with the practice for years and had recently become a partner. He examined Crystal who still couldn't get up, and confirmed my diagnosis.

'Milk fever,' he said. 'No doubt about it. We'll treat her for that and hopefully she'll get up in her own good time but I have to admit I don't like the look of that leg she's lying on, it's worrying.' The vet told us not to move her.

'Leave her lying quietly and when the injection I've given her begins to take effect hopefully she'll get up on her own. I'll come back later to see how she's getting on.'

David injected Crystal with a calcium preparation for her milk fever, washed his hands and left.

David returned at 5pm and Crystal looked much better. Obviously the calcium injection had cured her milk fever but she still hadn't attempted to stand.

We encouraged her and four or five of us pushed her. She tried to get to her feet but she just swayed and dragged her right back leg. She managed to get into our building but she immediately fell into the straw. Fortunately she fell with her troublesome leg on top, not underneath.

David examined the leg and came to the conclusion she had damaged and probably ruptured the muscles.

He injected her with painkillers and steroids and moved her to try to take some of the weight off her muscles. Then all we could do was wait and hope she would make progress.

Surrounded by pupils, Susan was quick to ask the question which we all dreaded.

'What happens if she doesn't make progress?'

'Then it would be kinder to have her put down,' David told her gently, adding that he would return next day.

She ate well when we held her bowl close to her and she also drank plenty of water.

The next morning we were all concerned when we saw she was still the same. We again managed to move her to take some of the weight off her muscles – it was this weight which was damaging them even more.

She ate and drank but made no attempt to stand.

David called again during the late afternoon – examined her again and gave her some more painkillers and steroids. Unfortunately there were no changes.

As time went by and Crystal made no attempt to get up I reluctantly had to face up to the fact that to all intents and

Milk Fever And Disaster

purposes we were going to lose her. David called again the next day for the fourth and final time. She had made no improvement and we were told to have her humanely destroyed.

That evening after school when all the students had gone home I arranged for Dennis Hayes to come in and get the job over and done with.

I was glad the pupils were not there to see her lifeless body being taken away on Dennis's lorry.

It was one of the saddest episodes in the history of the school farm.

The pupils were extremely upset. They cleaned out her building and then started collecting photographs of her.

Eleanor, one of my senior students, collected her milk records, wrote down her history and put the photos in order.

She got together with about twenty other students and they wrote an excellent letter which was addressed to HM Queen Elizabeth II, Buckingham Palace, London. They showed me the letter and I checked it for spelling mistakes, commas and any misplaced punctuation marks.

The letter told the Queen all about Crystal, how we bought her as a calf from the Royal Farm at Windsor and how we became the smallest officially recorded herd in Great Britain – we had only one cow.

Photographs illustrated our show successes and calves produced.

The letter also invited the Queen to visit us at our school farm. My students also sent a copy of my book 'Ducks In Detention' which has two chapters all about Crystal, one which includes buying her at the Royal Farms.

We then waited for a reply.

Chapter Five
It's Enough To Make A Bishop Swear

Hawthorn Jenny 2nd, Harry the Hoover's mother, was due to give birth again. This caused great excitement among the pupils as she was one of their favourites, a noisy individual and boss of all the ewes.

'I wonder if we'll get another Harry the Hoover,' pondered Susan. One of my fifth-year pupils, she could remember Harry very well. He had been sold to another farm and was now used for breeding purposes – he had about fifty ewes to serve if his new owners could only stop him eating. Harry seemed to be under the impression that his sole purpose in life was to clear as much food as possible in the shortest space of time. So much so that he frightened the life out of us one day. He was so ill his pitiful baas almost had us crying along with him. He was ill because he had eaten hundreds of damsons. He had given himself a kingsize stomach ache and nearly killed himself.

At about 2pm one Wednesday afternoon in March Jenny 2nd gave birth, with no assistance from me, to a good ram lamb.

'Harry the Hoover has a little brother,' I announced proudly to my regular helpers as they came to tend and feed the livestock. They had finished their lessons for the day so there was plenty of time for them to 'ooh' and 'aah' over the new baby.

'Has he drunk and drunk and drunk till he was ready to burst?' asked Susan. 'You know, like Harry the Hoover.'

'No he hasn't.' I shook my head. 'He seems quite normal at present.'

The black patches around their eyes and the black on their noses have become bigger on the modern-day Kerry Hill sheep and so the faces have more black and most of the ears are now black. These sheep usually fetch a better price at auction and do better in the shows than the ones with less black.

Rabbits On Report

Our newborn lamb was well marked and a good size, weighing in at twelve pounds. However, he was born late. Some of our other lambs were born two months earlier.

As usual we kept Jenny and her lamb in a lambing, or mothering-up pen, as they are called. Here they will get to know each other, staying for about three days before being put into a larger group of ewes and lambs.

The young lambs are super to watch, running, playing, jumping into the air, forming gangs and all running together. Ram lambs sometimes spoil things and have a habit of playing at mating with the other lambs. The average person doesn't realise they do this and they always, without exception, did it when I was showing some distinguished guests around the school. They, of course, went away with a very different idea about lambs, realising they are not as they are usually portrayed in children's farmyard books.

On the Saturday afternoon when the new lamb was old enough Jo carried him (closely followed by his mother) and placed him gently on the floor in the part of the building where the older groups of ewes and lambs were all together. He took a quick look around him – ignored his mother – ran straight to the nearest ewe lamb and immediately jumped on top of her and played at serving her.

'Look at him, sir,' said Michael, wide eyed with amazement. 'How old is he?'

'Three days,' I replied, equally stunned.

The ewe lamb was a lot bigger than he was and she ran off leaving him standing. Not to be outdone he tried it again but this time with a ram lamb. This lamb was also a good deal bigger than he was and he ran from underneath him, turned around and butted him so hard he fell to the floor. He got up, shook himself and trotted back to his mother for reassurance and had a drink from her.

If Harry the Hoover had a one-track mind his little brother was about to outdo him.

When we looked at the ewes and lambs again that afternoon the first thing we all saw was this ram lamb with a little ewe lamb smaller than himself. He was on her back – she kept moving to get out of the way – but he persisted.

'I can't believe this,' said Michael, shaking his head.

'No I can't either,' agreed Carol. 'He's such a cute little thing and only three days old. My Enid Blyton books never mentioned anything like this.'

'Lambs never behaved like that in my children's farmyard books either, or on television,' I added.

I could have bitten my tongue out as soon as I said it. I knew, for certain, I had definitely said the wrong thing. With a sly look Carol said, 'I can't imagine you as a child in short trousers, sir.'

'You can bet it was a long time ago,' said Susan. 'Can you remember the First World War?'

'I can't remember the Second, let alone the First.' It was time to change the subject, so before they could embarrass or insult me any more I said with authority, 'Let's get that empty lambing pen cleaned out.'

The lamb was now at it again – another ewe lamb was receiving his unwanted attentions. My pupils didn't want to clean out the lambing pen.

'Sir, look at him, he's at it again.'

'He's going to make a first-class breeding ram one day,' I said.

When the lamb was about three weeks old he became craftier. The ewes and lambs get fed with concentrated feed twice a day, eating from a metal sheep trough. This lamb would wait until all the others had got their heads down and then sneak up behind them and play at mating with the other lambs instead of eating. This was the complete opposite of his older brother Harry the Hoover. Harry lived to eat, now we had a Casanova on our hands.

At a month old he was trying it on with the ewes. They would have none of it. They certainly didn't want a 'toy boy' and made it quite clear by turning on him and butting him. He had more than one sheep equivalent of a good hiding but it didn't deter him.

It was soon time to take the ewes and lambs to our rented field situated nearby and owned by David and Jill Price. We hadn't seen David and Jill for four months and I was looking forward to seeing them again. The pupils and myself checked the fence to make sure there were no gaps or holes in it. Then we spread some fertiliser on the field and left it.

I had sold Jill a ewe and her lamb the previous year. This ewe was in lamb again to a neighbour's Suffolk ram. Her lamb, which had been born the previous year, hadn't been put to the ram, on my advice, because she was too small. These two sheep were indoors, not in the field. The field had been rested all winter and there was plenty of grass on it. The rain would soon wash the fertiliser in and it would grow lusher and greener. I filled the water tank but before I turned the sheep and lambs out into the field we wormed them all. The ewes' feet were in good condition and didn't need paring because I made a practice of paring each ewe while she was in the individual lambing pen. I did this as part of a lesson and over the years it proved very worthwhile.

When moving sheep and lambs I separate them in our trailer by putting the lambs on the top deck and the ewes on the bottom. That way the lambs don't get crushed by the ewes.

I took the ewes and lambs to the field in two journeys but one of our ewes had lambed only the day before so she stayed at the school. There were five ewes still left to lamb so they stayed behind as well.

All was going smoothly until a couple of days later when the telephone rang.

'Hello, is that John?'

'Speaking. That sounds like Jill,' I replied pleasantly.

'It is,' said a stony voice.

My heart stood still. I seemed to hear Lord Clifton's voice saying 'I have some terrible news for you' but then I pulled myself together. (I had worked on Lord Clifton's farms when I was a boy, and more recently kept sheep on his land and on more than one occasion he had telephoned me with bad news.) Perhaps she had called to tell me her ewe had lambed or, at worst, our sheep had got out and were being escorted back by the local constabulary. It wouldn't be the first time.

'What's the matter Jill, have our sheep got out and caused a nuisance?' I asked.

'No John, but I am so disgusted with one of them.'

It's Enough To Make A Bishop Swear

'Why? What has he or she done?' I asked innocently but secretly knew what was coming.

'Not he or she,' she said sternly. 'Him! Just one little lamb. I repeat – one little, supposedly innocent, lamb.'

She sounded really icy. This wasn't a happy lady I was talking to. There was a distinct growl in the word 'innocent'.

'Whatever is the matter Jill?' I asked ingenuously.

'Don't you come the innocent with me John Terry. You know fine well what's the matter. It's that ram lamb of yours. He's a complete disgrace. Did you know he was a psychopath?'

'Oh! That one! I think I know the one you mean.'

'Yes, I'm quite sure you do. My little god-daughter Julie came to stay with us at the weekend and I took her to show her the lambs. She thought it was wonderful because the older sheep took bread out of her hands and she loved watching the little ones gambolling about until he started his antics. He spoiled everything. That poor little girl didn't know what to make of it. "What's he doing, Auntie?" she asked. I told her, "Don't you take any notice of him, you just watch the others, he's being a silly boy," I said. "Yes but Auntie, what's he doing?" she kept asking. Now, you tell me, how do I explain that kind of behaviour to a little child? I can tell you it wasn't funny. I could have died of embarrassment.'

I tried to placate her.

'It's all very well being sorry but what are you going to do about him?'

'What can I do?' I asked, at a loss for what to say.

'Castrate him,' came the short sharp reply.

'Well, I can only apologise again,' I said. 'I know the lamb you mean, he does seem to have a one-track mind.'

'Yes, a damn dirt track,' came the prompt reply. 'I really didn't know what to tell our Julie. If you don't castrate the dirty little devil I will when I get hold of him.'

Suddenly visions of Mick and his penknife flitted through my mind. I apologised once more and asked her if her ewe had lambed. She hadn't.

I told my pupils about their lamb and his carryings on.

'Let's call him Randy Dandy,' suggested Susan.

We all laughed at this suggestion but agreed it suited him down to the ground. I had called a ram Randy Dandy many years earlier; however, he was nothing compared with this new lamb.

A few days later, in desperation Jill resorted to a bucket of cold water but even that didn't cool his ardour. Unfortunately, she soaked the poor little ewe lamb who must have wondered what on earth she had done to merit such treatment. Jill then had the idea of turning the hosepipe on him. That worked. He didn't like that one bit. The strong jet of water was too much even for him. But it didn't last long. People who think sheep are stupid should think again. It didn't take this one long to work out that if he got up a good head of steam when he saw Jill coming and put distance between them he would be out of her range and could perform further down the field. He was not yet old enough to be fertile (which was more than could be said for his imagination) so he really was just a shameless nuisance without doing any real damage. Also, our breed of ewes only came on heat in the late summer or autumn so he wouldn't get any in lamb. But you could almost hear them saying 'Clear off you little pest.'

Jill's ewe gave birth to a little ewe lamb which was fine.

'That, that creature of yours had better keep away from my ewe lamb,' said Jill protectively 'or so help me I'll give him something to be going on with. I'll give him a smack he won't forget in a hurry.'

You'd think the lamb was her teenage daughter.

I had entered a ram lamb for the Royal Show at Stoneleigh but was unsure of which one to take. My pupils caught half a dozen in the field and most of us agreed it had to be Randy Dandy. He was, by far, the best ram lamb we had. We bathed and shampooed him a month before the show, he was then carded and trimmed each week, halter trained – revelling all the while in the extra attention – and came fourth at the show. He had good, distinctive markings, he had no brown or grey on his face, his ears were erect, he had good teeth and walked well. What let him down was his size. Most of his rivals had been born in February or March.

He was born in early April – he was just younger. He had not disgraced us by coming last and I knew he would grow into a large sheep. It augured well for the future.

'How did Randy Dandy get on at the show?' asked David.

'Fourth prize,' I replied.

'Oh! I thought he'd do better,' he said.

'He was too small – most of the other lambs were older and so larger than him. A good big one will always beat a good little one,' I declared, quoting an expression I had heard many times from my rival exhibitors.

'Well it's no wonder he's too small. You're not surprised are you? After all he never stands still long enough to put on any weight, and we all know why, don't we? He's too busy doing what comes naturally,' he said meaningfully.

'Yes. I can't argue with that,' I agreed.

'The other lambs have put on pounds since he's been out of the field and their nerves have settled down a lot. They lead a much calmer life without him after them all the time. They don't have to keep looking over their shoulder to see if Don Juan is on the prowl.'

I laughed. He continued, 'Do you know, I have actually witnessed him trying to mate with his own mother.'

'So have I,' I said.

'He definitely wants castrating,' said Jill who had just joined us.

'He needs it but I don't think he wants it,' I said flippantly, earning myself a black look. 'No, be fair, he'll make a first-class breeding ram one day.'

'Well you can't say his heart isn't in it,' laughed David. 'I supposed he served everything in sight at the Royal Show, did he?'

'No, actually he didn't. He was penned on his own and couldn't get out.'

'A-ha. Reputation gone before him?'

'It's a good job he couldn't get out from what I've seen of him' rejoined Jill. 'I warn you now John, if that sex-mad psychopath so much as looks at my little darling I'll give him what for. I'll knock damn spots off him.'

'You can't do that Jill,' I said in mock alarm. 'We need

those to show his pedigree.'

'Oh I'll show him his pedigree all right. He can have his pedigree hanging on blue ribbons over his pen and he can look at it all day,' she threatened.

The trouble is, I think she meant it. He certainly wasn't Jill's flavour of the month. Dish of the day maybe. I think she would love to have seen him surrounded by roast potatoes and with a liberal dash of mint sauce.

After the show Dandy had to go back in the field for a few weeks. He still hadn't calmed down. Much to his chagrin the ewes had gone but to compensate there were plenty of lambs for him to chase. However, before the autumn the ram lambs were separated from the ewe lambs, an action which produced a big sulk.

He was to live with the other two show hopefuls, both rams. They were the tops in our flock that would compete in the shows next year. He wasn't the largest one of the three, in fact, although he was the middle one he would pick a fight with the other two or else try to mate with them, an action guaranteed to start a brawl. It didn't bother Dandy that they were not of the opposite sex.

He though all his birthdays had come at once though when he saw all the ewes at the autumn dipping. All the sheep were together but it was only for a few minutes and we soon scotched any evil plan he might have been harbouring by putting him in a pen just for rams. This wasn't what he had in mind at all. He made a complete and utter nuisance of himself, charging, fighting and generally upsetting them all. It had become a full-time job for us keeping law and order so we pulled him out, dipped him and penned him on his own after which he quietened down for half an hour or so. Sulking again, no doubt.

He was then put back with the other two rams. Then one day his big chance came. William, our stock ram, was not getting all our ewes in lamb. He had served them, leaving a raddle mark but then half of them came on heat again sixteen or seventeen days later. He served these ewes again but I didn't want to leave it to him so it would be good stockmanship to use another ram. Randy Dandy seemed the obvious choice out of the three show rams. We had never used a ram lamb for breeding before so we were in uncharted waters, but at least he was dedicated to the job. We fitted him out with a raddle and crayon. I caught William and put him in the trailer. He wasn't pleased. Another sulker.

I turned Dandy loose and as he raced away I could swear I heard aloud 'Yee hah, Geronimo.' I half-expected to hear 'Remember the Alamo' but I don't think history was his strong point. The future was more to his liking, especially the future of the Kerry Hill breed. But look at it, all that fun and no Jill and hosepipe. Within seconds of release he had served a ewe. He didn't mess about, this lad. You couldn't say he wasn't keen.

Actually, we had misjudged poor William, he hadn't done so badly after all. Out of twenty-four ewes he had got twenty in lamb. The other four were all Dandy's. I'm sure he was disappointed that there wasn't more work for him. Unfortunately one of the four was his own mother, Hawthorn Jenny 2nd.

On Christmas Eve I took him out from the ewes and he was sheared along with the other two rams and four ewe lambs. He would now stay indoors until the spring. He was now well and truly away from the ewes and he was fretting for them. He was missing them so much that one morning he messed in his feed trough. I knelt down to clean it out and I felt a large heavy weight on my back – it was him. Likewise sometime later we were cleaning out his pen when he climbed on top of the wheelbarrow. Mr Petty, our woodwork teacher, fell about laughing when he heard this and suggested I put some rubber stoppers on the wheelbarrow handles to stop his game, either that or he would get some of the boys in his class to turn some wood bungs similar to those used in beer barrels.

On Valentine's Day one group of pupils was outside working on their projects when such a commotion broke out. I looked out of the window to see what all the fuss was about and saw Katie charging full steam ahead along the path towards the classroom waving her arms about and shouting in real panic. Now, Katie, to put it politely, was a well-built girl and I didn't realise anyone her size could move so fast. She literally barnstormed in, crashing the door open and yelled 'Sir, sir – Jemma 4th has lambed.'

I just stood looking blankly at her.

'What?' I asked in disbelief. 'She can't have – not yet. You're having me on.'

'No sir, I'm not. Honestly, she has lambed.'

Her wide eyes and shocked white face were enough to convince me that she was telling the truth. She ran back outside waving her arms wildly in the air. I followed to where our sheep were. We had them split into early lambing and late lambing groups. Jemma 4th was in the late lambing group and according to our records not due for about another six weeks, in fact, we had nothing due for at the earliest, another three weeks. But, there he was, a good strong ram lamb, already on his feet and looking for the milk bar. His markings were excellent – a future champion maybe?

'I can't understand it – there is nothing due to lamb until three weeks' time, let alone this one – it's not possible.' The word had got around and the rest of the group, all eager to see the new arrival, surrounded me.

'Is the lamb premature?' asked Katie.

'No, not a chance. Look at the size of him, he's a big lamb.'

We checked him over. We had already seen him drinking.

It's Enough To Make A Bishop Swear

We gave him a clean bill of health and then immediately put iodine on his navel to stop joint ill.

Suddenly it dawned on me.

'I've got it,' I cried excitedly. 'It's Randy Dandy. I'd like to bet he served this ewe on dipping day. Can you remember he was chasing the ewes and causing such pandemonium we had to take him out of the way? It looks as if we weren't quick enough. I didn't see him serve this ewe but it certainly looks like it.'

'It could be,' said Neil who was normally a shy boy but was brought out of his shell by the excitement of the newborn lamb. We went and consulted the farm diary, the sheep were dipped on 20 September, exactly 147 days to Valentine's Day – Dandy was the culprit. He hadn't been sulking that day he had been quietly gloating. The so-and-so had scored one over us that time. Game, set and match to him.

'We could call the lamb Valentine,' suggested Carol.

'Excellent idea,' I said and everyone agreed.

Randy Dandy also served his own mother and got her in lamb. She lambed at the end of the season, it was a single ram lamb and the best ram lamb to be born in the year. This is a prime example of in-breeding when an ancestor is common to both parents, when the son is put to the mother or brother to sister. It is not recognised practice for the ordinary farmer. It could breed the best qualities in stock – but it can also bring out the bad qualities – some of which are harmful.

'It's incest really,' quipped Michael. 'And it looks as if it runs in their family.' He indicated Dandy and his mother.

A lady visitor to the farm, who was actually a school governor, on hearing of the amorous adventures of our naughty boy remarked, 'Your wool ought to be black.' Dandy glowered at her, lowered his head and butted the gate to his pen. 'You headcase,' our visitor said, 'you'll give yourself a migraine.' This exchange of pleasantries resulted in a staring contest. The two protagonists glared at each other, each trying to make the other back down and lose face, so to speak. Dandy won. I knew he would because at his most belligerent that ram could outstare a glass eyeball. We left his shed with a triumphant 'Baa' ringing in our ears. Or was it 'Bah'.

Time went by and he had been entered for all the shows which we attended. His first as a shearling was to be the Shropshire and West Midland at Shrewsbury. It was a two-day show – Wednesday and Thursday. We always liked to take our sheep up in the evening before the show to get them settled in. Pupils and myself got a move on, feeding the livestock then loading up the trailer with the show sheep – a pair of shearling ewes called Belinda and Beth, Dandy and another shearling ram called Jack. Dandy tried to mate with one of the ewes within seconds of entering the trailer. I couldn't get on the road quick enough. I was worried to death in case he injured the ewes because his attentions were definitely unwelcome; he could also get their backs dirty with his hooves and they were in pristine condition. Once travelling we were all right, until we stopped at the first set of traffic lights. We sat waiting for them to change when suddenly the trailer went into a rock'n'roll sequence. Everyone walking by was giving us strange looks.

'Do you think the trailer's come off?' asked John.

'I wouldn't think so, no. It's more likely to be Randy Dandy,' exclaimed Carol.

'It's sure to be,' I confirmed.

There was nothing we could do about it but just sit there and look as if it were quite normal for a trailer to be dancing about the road as if a demented trampolinist was inside. Then at the showground we had to queue to get in. Oh wasn't that great, suited him down to the ground – he was at it again.

At the show I left him and Jack in the adjoining pens. I made sure the ewes were in the pen next to Jack (much to their profound relief I suspect). I couldn't trust Dandy, if there were ewes next to him he would probably jump over and have his wicked way with them whether they liked it or not. I wouldn't have put it past him to jump into Jack's pen and then move over into the ewes. The other worrying thing was that on the other side of him was an empty pen, which would soon contain Mr Williamson's sheep. I was wondering what he would put in the pen next to Dandy and I fervently hoped it would be a ram. Even so, that wouldn't stop him but at least he might get a good head butt. I just couldn't trust him.

I went home, dropping the three pupils off at their homes and we met again at 5am the next morning. After feeding the livestock at the school we travelled to the show for the judging.

The sheep were fine but to my dismay there were two ewes in the pen next to Dandy. I studied the pen and decided he would never jump over, the hurdles were too high and the pen too small for him to get a good run at it.

I gave all our sheep a quick card and trim and then it was judging time. The ewes did very well – second prize and they went on to be reserve female champions. Dandy was first and Jack third.

After lunch we came back to find Dandy had started to demolish his pen. He had head-butted the wooden hurdles so hard that some of the wooden rails were now on the floor with nails sticking dangerously up in the air; he was in danger of stepping on one at any moment. It was obvious he couldn't jump over to the two ewes so it seemed he had every intention of battering his way through. Suddenly, he backed into the very far corner of his pen, put his head down and charged the remaining rails. With a tooth jarring thud his head connected with the rails and there was a loud cracking noise. One of the rails splintered in two but it didn't hurt him – he was a real Rambo of the sheep world. I jumped into the pen before he could give an action replay. The two ewes were terrified. They were barging about in their own pen and then they moved into the far corner, away from Dandy. I caught Dandy, put a halter on him and tied him to the corner of his pen.

I was joined by pupils Michael and Carol.

'I see he's been up to his old tricks again,' observed Carol.

'Good grief, sir. He's got his own demolition outfit,' said Michael.

'The stewards are going to love him. He's wrecked half the showground,' Carol said.

'I've told you a million and one times not to exaggerate,' said Michael in fun.

'Yes, all right you two, don't go on about it, I'm well aware of what he's done,' I said a little irritably.

Robert Porter came over to have a look.

'Whoops. He's made a good job of that,' he observed. 'What's he done that for? Is he claustrophobic?'

I inclined my head towards the ewes' pen. 'It's those two,' I answered.

'Women,' chipped in Michael who, at thirteen, considered himself to be something of an authority on the subject.

Robert bit back a smile and said 'Oh!'

'I don't suppose you would have a hammer in your lorry would you?' I asked.

'I have.'

'Can I borrow it please?'

'You can and I suppose you want me to fetch it?'

'Yes please.'

He was soon back with the hammer and thoughtfully brought some nails as well which would save time trying to straighten the old ones. Have you ever tried to straighten used nails? It's not the easiest task in the world. Then I had to set about mending the pen. I was closely watched by Robert. He didn't offer to help – why should he? He'd supplied the hammer and nails, labour was extra. He was checking my woodwork skills – could a teacher be practical as well? I therefore did my best to turn out some first-class work, then, after all my efforts he never said a damn word.

I put the hurdle back in place but knowing Dandy it wouldn't take long for him to smash it down again. I had to find an alternative, something that would stand up to Dandy's onslaught. I spotted a pile of metal hurdles. I helped myself and carried them back to the pen. I replaced the wooden hurdles with the metal ones and let Attila the Hun off his halter. He wandered over to the new rails, sniffed them, decided they were too strong and capitulated.

However, when we were loading the sheep up to go home on the Thursday evening I noticed one hurdle had actually got two bent bars in it. He'd had a go at the two bars after all, trying to get to the ewes. He must have given himself a thumping headache.

To our surprise he behaved admirably at the Royal Show and came first. He also behaved at the Royal Welsh, even though the judge only placed him second. Perhaps the crack on the head with the iron bars had knocked some sense in at last.

Judging was over by late Monday afternoon at the Royal Welsh but the show didn't finish until the Thursday. I arranged with Mr Williamson for him to feed the sheep for the duration of the show as I couldn't justify staying at the show for the other three days. I would be distracted thinking about all the jobs that needed doing at the school. I could hardly rest when away from the place. It meant extra mileage though. I would have to travel back 140 miles, then return on Thursday making it a round trip of 280 miles in one day.

I noticed a vicar tending his Southdown sheep.

'Hello,' I said.

'Good afternoon,' he replied in a clear, ringing voice.

'Tending your flock?' I asked cheekily.

'Yes, and they're a sight less trouble than some of my human ones I can tell you.'

After some chat it turned out the Reverend Hubbard only lived fifteen miles from my home.

My second cheeky question was, 'Is there any chance you could bring our sheep back to where you live?' I don't know what he thought of me but I explained the situation to him.

'Yes I can do that if you haven't got many.'

'Only three,' I replied, omitting to mention that one was a juvenile delinquent.

'Oh that's no problem. I can get three in the trailer.'

I showed him our sheep and he said he would telephone me when he arrived home and I could collect the sheep from there.

On the Thursday evening his wife telephoned me to tell me he had arrived home with the sheep. I had already hitched up the trailer and was soon on my way to the vicarage. I found it easily enough – a large ivy-clad house set back off the road with a long drive sweeping in and out.

I got out of the car and walked towards the door – it opened before I could ring the bell. The Reverend Hubbard stood framed in the doorway with a face like thunder. I could see he was absolutely furious. A vicar angry? Was that possible? Yes it was.

'Hello there. Thanks for bringing the sheep back,' I said.

'It's enough to make a bishop swear,' he said, ignoring my opening gambit.

'Oh dear. Whatever is the matter?' I asked, putting on my innocent choirboy look which fooled no one for an instant.

'I think you know what the matter is. Why didn't you tell me that ram of yours is a sex-mad lunatic? He had a fight with my Southdown ram, almost knocking him cross-eyed and loosening every tooth in his head then he had the damned effrontery to mate with my two ewes.'

'Oh! I see ...' but before I could say any more he carried on. 'Every time I stopped for traffic lights the trailer started aerobic dancing. I'm sure your ram was trying to mate with my ewes even then. I felt so ashamed. Everyone was looking.'

'I'm so sorry. He does seem to have a bit of a problem.'

'A bit of a problem! He's got a gigantic problem. He needs a psychiatrist – or a sharp knife.'

We walked over to the Reverend Hubbard's trailer. The Southdowns had been put safely away: one battered, shell-shocked and with a splitting headache and possibly toothache as well and two rape cases. I wondered which ward they were in and if I should send some flowers.

I backed our trailer up to the back of his, we lowered the ramp and transferred our three from his trailer to mine.

'How much do I owe you?' I asked.

'Nothing for the moment,' he snapped, 'but if my two prize-winning ewes are in lamb you will have a hefty bill to pay.'

On the way home I began to wonder what his sermon for the following Sunday would be: 'Love Thy neighbour' or 'The Seven Deadly Sins'. 10–1 he wouldn't choose 'Little Lamb Who Made Thee.' Or 'Oh please to keep thy loving eye on all poor creatures born to die' from Dylan Thomas's play 'Under Milk Wood' because at that moment Dandy was top of his hitlist. Deep down I felt sorry for the poor man. He had been doing us a favour when all's said and done. Randy Dandy had let us down in more ways than one. He had broken more than one of the ten commandments.

Dandy went to a few more shows in the summer. He was then fed well to 'build steam' and was promoted to stock ram status. He was put in the field with twenty-four pedigree Kerry Hill ewes. His heart and soul was in his career and it wasn't long before all two dozen of them were in lamb. He was a very unlikely hero but you couldn't help admiring him but then, in a school full of characters what was one more?

Chapter Six
Dipping Time

I have always been a great admirer of the Kerry Hill breed of sheep and I was so proud of our own flock. With their distinctive markings of black patches around each eye and the nose, black ears and legs they looked as if they could be distant relatives of the giant panda and who can resist that lovely animal? The fleece on the Kerry Hill should be good and free from any black patches although in reality some lambs are born with a black patch in their necks.

Kerry Hill ewes make marvellous mothers, giving plenty of milk to feed the lambs. The breed is a good commercial proposition with lambs that mature into first-class meat. They are hardy and particularly resistant to disease.

Sheep are excellent animals to use in a school. There were so many rural studies lessons in which I could use them, such as showing the characteristics of mammals, wool production, meat production, shearing, trimming for shows, showing, feet trimming, pests and diseases, feeding, general stockmanship, pedigree breeding involving genetics and actual lambing.

We kept some wonderful sheep over the years, breeding from some selected individuals to try and get the best. We had families of Jennys, Jemmas, Lisas, Lindas, Susies and Katies. They were named in sequence so, for instance, if Jenny 3rd gave birth to a ewe lamb good enough to register, the lamb was called Jenny 4th and so on. Our ram lambs were given any name that appeared to suit them – Randy Dandy for instance. Now there was one ram that really did live up to his name.

I was showing a group of older students how we had selected individuals of the Linda family, showing them the latest Linda. She was the best of all and our best ram, unrelated to her, which was Randy Dandy, would serve her.

'Randy Dandy will enjoy that, sir. I bet he likes a new, young girlfriend instead of some of the old grannies he has to serve,' said Robert.

'It's all the same to him,' I replied. 'He's the one that got his own mother in lamb and tried to mate with the wheelbarrow'.

'That's why you've put rubber stoppers on the handles of the wheelbarrow isn't it, sir?' remarked Phillip.

'That's correct,' I said.

I should have seen where all this was leading but no, I opened the floodgates of 'What do you get ... etc.'

'What do you get if you cross a sheep with a wheelbarrow?' asked Karen.

'I don't know, what do you get if you cross a sheep with a wheelbarrow?' I replied.

'I don't know either but I'm sure you'll come up with something before the end of the lesson,' she responded.

'I expect so,' I replied conceitedly. 'In the meantime what do you get if you cross a dog with a cockerel? Any offers? Does anyone know?' I asked.

There was silence (unusual for them) and a lot of frowns and puzzled looks.

'Give in? It's a poodle that cocks its own doodle'.

This got a very mixed reaction. Most of them laughed, one or two groaned and others pulled a face.

'Do you know any more, sir?'

'Well there was a geneticist that crossed a haddock with a toadstool and produced a packet of fish fungus.'

More groans and fewer laughs this time.

'Any more, sir?' asked Susan.

'There was a fellow who crossed a Morse code transmitter with a laxative and got three dots and a very quick dash.'

Blank stares and more groans greeted this one. Some got it, others didn't.

'I know one,' said Glyn excitedly. 'A scientist crossed a cockerel with a banjo and got a chicken that plucks itself.'

The class roared with laughter.

'That's a better one than yours, sir.'

I could see which road we were going down, the more puns and jokes that were cracked the less work they would have to do. It was time to call a halt to the jollity. They were still howling with laughter when the door opened and there stood Mr Beech framed in the doorway.

'What's the joke?' he asked.

'We were just discussing selective breeding,' I replied seriously.

'Oh really! Not much humour there I would have thought,' he said. 'I'll leave you to it then.' And with that he went out and everyone breathed a sigh of relief.

At last the serious business of the day got underway with Claire telling the class that her parents bred pedigree Labradors and she told the class how they had selected various dogs and bitches for showing. This all proved very interesting and I learned something too.

Another student, Stuart, said his grandad had grown and selected the most enormous pumpkins but they were so big and heavy the lifting had given him a rupture so now he was specialising in cucumbers instead.

'Has he developed any new strains?' I asked.

The lesson was rapidly drawing to a close and I still hadn't thought of a line for what do you get when you cross a sheep with a wheelbarrow. In desperation I clutched at straws.

'I know what you get if you cross a sheep with a wheelbarrow,' I cried. 'It's a sheep you can push around and when it goes to the loo it goes straight into the barrow.'

The groans that greeted this remark were unanimous.

'Good grief, sir, is that the best you can come up with?'

'Scraping the bottom of the barrel aren't you, sir?'

Maybe they were right but it was the best I could do at the time.

One job with the sheep that I didn't get the whole class involved in was dipping. Every sheep farmer in England was required by law to carry out a statutory dipping programme on all their sheep twice a year, once in the summer and again in the autumn. The dipping was done within certain dates specified by MAFF – the Ministry of Agriculture, Fisheries and Food. All sheep had to be dipped, except those going for slaughter, within the dipping period.

Nowadays all sheep are sprayed with a safer alternative to the organophosphorous sheep dip which is now recognised as a health hazard to the dippers.

In previous years, to save costs, I would get together with Jim Finney, using his sheep-dipping bath and pens. We would buy the appropriate sheep dip between us and both dip on the same day. Now, however, we had so many sheep I felt it was time to dip ours on a different day to Jim.

I telephoned Jim to ask if we could take our sheep to his farm and dip them. He agreed and I told him the best day for me would be the following Saturday. I couldn't do the job on a weekday because it meant I would need another teacher to cover my lessons and I couldn't see Mr Beech agreeing to that. He didn't mind so much when we were showing as any wins reflected well on the school but just to dip a 'lot of smelly sheep' as he put it, wouldn't go down too well.

Sheep were dipped mainly to ward off sheep scab. Two different mites cause this nasty affliction which causes the sheep to lose their wool and thick scabs or scabs surrounded by moist or wet rings appear. The sheep scratch themselves and rub against posts, fences, trees or any other hard surface available, even the corners of walls. Anything to get some relief. Sheep scab was eradicated from Britain by sheep dipping but then outbreaks occurred over a wide area, hence the eradication campaign organised by the Ministry.

Sheep dipping also helped to control another uninvited parasite: the blowfly. These unpleasant little intruders lay their eggs in dirty moist wool, usually under the tail. Sheep with diarrhoea or scouring as it is called, are prone to flies in muggy weather. The eggs hatch into maggots which eat the flesh of the sheep. The sheep are very unsettled if they have maggots, wagging their tails and scratching a lot. It is important to keep the sheep's hind quarters clean by cutting off any dirty wool – this is called dagging. Dipping the sheep also kills off lice, ticks and other fairly common external parasites of sheep – all extremely unpleasant. At one time dipping was the only remedy and had to be done.

Dipping Time

Jim had a good sheep-dipping set-up. It was a metal tank set in concrete with a holding pen at the front of the bath and a draining pen at the other end. Because the floor of the pens and the tank surround was concrete the sheep took very little soil or muck into the dip with them. The draining pen floor sloped backwards into the bath so the water and sheep dip drained out of the sheep's coat and back into the tank.

Having got Jim's permission I filled in the relevant form to give five clear days' notice in writing to my local authority – Warwickshire County Council. It was at a time when I was feeling run down and tired. It was getting towards the end of term and I had been busy with examinations, reports and parents' evenings. We had also had a heavy showing season having shown at the Shropshire and West Midland Show, Montgomeryshire, Three Counties and the Royal, winning prizes in all of them. Showing is hard work and very draining. Most of us were running on reserve energy and we were by no means finished. There were another eleven shows including the Royal Welsh and the Town and Country remaining. Suddenly it looked as if life might get a bit easier when one of my former pupils, Janet, put in an appearance wanting to help.

Janet had been one of my star pupils and she always kept in touch, visiting the school to see how the department was developing. She had always been one of my most enthusiastic workers, especially with the livestock, in fact she was the first pupil ever to show sheep for us. That was in 1981 at the Shropshire and West Midland. We were real amateurs in those days and had a lot to learn but we were placed fifth at the show and felt quite pleased with ourselves.

After leaving school Janet did a full-time course at the Warwickshire College of Agriculture at Moreton Morrell near Warwick. She had worked on a few farms including taking a full-time job with Matt Corbutt. At this farm she was in charge of a flock of ewes. Matt would buy old cross-breed ewes in the autumn and put them to his Suffolk ram. Lambing would then start in April. The ewes with their lambs would be sold when the lambs looked good and strong at a month or six weeks old. They would be sold on and then Matt would buy some more old ewes the following autumn.

Janet was also a competent tractor driver, working in shifts with Matt. I have known Janet to plough all night then be taken off by Matt at 8am the next morning. Not many girls would do that.

Warwickshire County Council, after a great deal of persuasion on my part, had agreed, at last, to let me have a part-time stock person for whom it would pay the wages. I had completed years without missing a single feed including Saturdays, Sundays, Christmas Day, Boxing Day, Bank holidays and the morning after the night before, sometimes feeling like death on legs. The stockperson's job was certainly 'part time' – four hours a week was all it was. This would give me two feeds a week off, either Saturday or Sunday. Alternatively I could 'save' the hours and the person could work eight hours one weekend and none the next, or, if I had a skilled job to do that needed two of us we could work together.

The years had passed since Janet worked for Matt Corbutt and in that time she had married and given birth to a little boy. I was glad she had been to see me, it would be good to have her working with our livestock again. She had done very well at college and with her experience at lambing ewes she was obviously the first person I turned to. It was such a pity she could only do four hours a week. I would have liked her help far more.

Her first skilled job with me was to be the dipping. It is a skilled job, it's not just a case of throwing the sheep in a bath of water and letting them swim for it. Everything has to be precise, the chemical measurements have to be accurate, the sheep have to be timed in the bath, every bit of them has to be immersed.

Janet and I got together and planned our strategy. We decided that she should stay at the dipping tank and dip the sheep while I transported the sheep to and fro.

Most of our sheep were at David Price's place. There were twenty Kerry Hill ewes with their lambs – thirty-one in all, and ten Clun Forest ewes with their seventeen Suffolk cross lambs. At school we had all the Kerry Hill show sheep, one two-year-old ram, two shearling rams and four shearling ewes making a grand total of eighty-five sheep to dip.

I went for my usual Friday night pint at our local – the Black Horse – on the evening before the dipping. There were quite a few farmers in the bar including Graham Wilson; the talk, naturally enough was of farming and little else.

'We are dipping the sheep tomorrow,' I said. 'And I'm hoping we don't get the man from the Ministry along to check if we are doing it correctly'.

'We've never had a visit from him,' Graham said casually.

'No? Well you've been jolly lucky then,' I replied.

'It's got nothing to do with luck.' He sipped his beer with such a smug look on his face.

'Well, are you going to tell us then or not?' I asked.

'It's the way my dad fills the form in, that's all. Dipping at Home Farm on Sunday 7 July at 11.30pm.' He moved his hand in a sweeping motion as if to indicate a banner hanging up in front of him. 'Do you think anyone in their right mind would turn out at that time of night, on a Sunday, to watch a few sheep take a swim?'

'Oh that's typical,' I snorted. 'Still, I've got to hand it to him. I would never have thought of that but then as a school teacher I don't think the officials would be very impressed if I did.'

My experience with the official is that he stands there without so much as getting a smut on his face and watches all that goes on. A few years ago when our sheep battered the holding pen fence down and ran off into Jim Finney's wheat did he offer to help? Did he ever? There wasn't so much as a whimper from him. He did, however, time the sheep in the dipping bath, making sure each one spent the statutory minute in the bath and that every bit was immersed.

One of our neighbours could certainly have done with an official on hand when he did his dipping because he got it completely wrong. Being new to sheep farming he thought the whole sheep had to be immersed for at least a whole minute. The poor things surfaced coughing and spluttering and gasping for breath. He almost had two expire on him before he cottoned on to his mistake.

Our show team of sheep were dipped before the shows, in a small tank at the school which was sufficient for them but would be of little use when dipping eighty-five.

Dipping day began fine and dry, the sky was crystal clear without a cloud in sight and it promised to be a scorcher. The sheep's wool would soon dry in the intense heat. I arranged with Janet that she would drive to Jim Finney's farm to fill the tank with clean water. 300ml of scab-approved dip would then be added to 450 litres of water. When handling dips and dipping the sheep overalls, rubber gloves and face masks had to be worn and she had collected these from the school a couple of days earlier.

Carol, Michael, Jo and Susan were my helpers. We quickly fed the livestock, finishing in a record time of fifteen minutes. Our first job after that was to load up the sheep that were housed at the school – our show team. These went in the dip first while it was clean – it is surprising how quickly the water becomes filthy after a few sheep have been through. We hitched up the trailer and loaded the seven sheep. They were used to being loaded and unloaded and it was just par for the course to them. They went in quietly enough and we were soon loaded up and ready to go. I was about to drive off when to my surprise another of my old pupils turned up. It was Daniel and I was delighted to see him. Could I 'Shanghai' him into helping today? I hadn't seen him for months but he was always a welcome visitor, always keen to lend a hand and got stuck into any task I gave him. He had left his job as a builder and gone back to farming, working, I discovered, for Ivor Shorthouse. He had grown into a fine strapping lad who practised weight lifting for a hobby.

'What are you doing today?' he asked.

'We are dipping today,' I replied.

'Mind if I come along? I'd like to help,' he said.

'You certainly can.'

Carol and Jo got into the back of the car while Daniel sat in the front passenger seat. Michael and Susan would have to wait at the school for the time being. We soon arrived at Jim Finney's farm. Janet sat on the fence waiting for us and as I approached I could see everything was ready.

'Oh good afternoon and what time to do you call this?' Janet joked. 'What kept you?'

'I'm early,' I said in self-defence.

'Early? I've been here ages and I'm ready to work.' Then as an afterthought, 'Hi Daniel.'

We unloaded the sheep into the holding pen. Janet and Daniel knew each other from school and could work well together. I took a large bundle of protective clothing out of the car boot. It included all the appropriate overalls, rubber gloves and wellingtons so that everyone working on the dipping would be protected.

I went into the house to tell Jim we had arrived – he said he would keep out of our way and let us get on with it. When I got back outside they were all 'gowned up' and ready to start. The two-year-old ram was first to go in, this was old hat to him and he was soon swimming. He was a big sheep and it took all Daniel's skill to keep him in the tank and force his head and ears under.

The sheep might be used to dipping but it didn't mean they had to like it and he came up baaing and protesting loudly. After the minute was up we let him out of the dip and he staggered up the slope. The weight of the water and dip was almost too much for him and for a few seconds his knees seemed to buckle under him. He hadn't been sheared since Christmas which was over six months ago so his fleece was long and heavy. The extra weight of the water in his wool brought him to a standstill. Fortunately it soon ran off him and back into the dip, after which he was fine. Then Janet grabbed a shearling ram and shouted to me, 'Go on, fetch the other sheep – you can trust us you know.'

'Stop looking so worried,' said Daniel. 'If one of them nearly drowns I'll give it the kiss of life.'

Jo was to be their timekeeper so I took them at their word and left them to it.

Carol came back to school with me to pick up Michael and Susan. The four of us then went to David Price's farm. We all rounded up the sheep – getting them into a holding pen that we had previously constructed with our hurdles. The decks, which turned the trailer into a double decker, were already in the trailer. We drove as many sheep as we could on to the top deck, secured it and then filled the bottom deck. Of course we couldn't get all the lambs with their mothers in the trailer. Some would be on the top deck, some on the bottom and some would be left in the pen for the second journey. Proceedings were rather noisy. There was such a din we could hardly hear ourselves think. Thank goodness it wouldn't be for long. Carol was to come with me to the dip; we both climbed into the car – it was a lot of weight for the car to pull so I drove extra carefully.

Once back at the Finneys I backed the trailer into position – this was a bit tricky because in front of the dip was a grassed area used by Mrs Finney as her drying ground. There was a line full of washing out and I didn't want a pair of her 'unmentionables' fluttering like a banner from the top of the trailer.

'Took your time didn't you?' said cheeky Janet again.

'I see you've finished,' I said. The show sheep were in the draining pens and they looked lovely and clean – whiter than before – which meant they looked striking. They should do well at the Royal Welsh Show, I thought.

'Any problems?' I asked.

'No. I didn't have to give any the kiss of life,' Daniel replied.

We unloaded our cargo of sheep. Those on the bottom came out first, then we lowered the ramp and out came the sheep off the top deck.

'Now we have plenty to do,' enthused Daniel. These ewes were sheared in June and so had only one month's growth of wool; they would be easier than the show sheep. Our show team had drained sufficiently and we loaded them back into the trailer. Janet and Daniel would dip again after the new sheep were rested.

I took the show sheep back to school on my own. I then drove to David's farm and loaded up the remaining sheep. Susan came back with me this time and we found them all working hard at the Finneys' farm. Daniel and Carol were catching the sheep and lowering them into the bath. Janet had a long pole which she used to keep the sheep in the bath, immersing their heads and ears once. Jo was timing each sheep with the stopwatch, making sure each one stayed in the bath for one minute.

Dipping stopped, I unloaded the next lot and loaded up the group that had just been dipped. Janet topped the dip up with more water and dip. This was done exactly according to the manufacturer's instructions – I could rely on her 100 percent to get it right.

I took the loaded sheep back to the farm and put them back in the field, then I loaded up the last lot out of the holding pen. Michael came back with me – he hadn't seen any dipping done and I thought it only fair that as he was on the team he should get the chance to see it. We had a spare set of protective clothes for him so he wouldn't be at any risk. We unloaded the last lot, loaded up the second lot and I took them back to their field on my own. The day was now very hot – sweltering in fact, the sky was a deep azure blue and there wasn't a breath of wind, the dippers must have been wringing with sweat under all that protective clothing.

They were all doing a grand job and I was proud to watch them for a few minutes even if they looked as though they had just landed from another planet.

'Come on, sir, you can join in if you want to,' called Jo.

'Hold on a minute, I thought it was agreed I was to be the transport manager.'

'We'll let you off this time,' remarked Michael.

'Oh well, that's very magnanimous of you,' I said.

'Oh here he goes with his big words again,' said Susan.

Just then Janet shouted, 'That's the last one.'

'That's the one we've been waiting for,' grinned Susan.

'No it's not. There's one more,' shouted Daniel.

We all looked round. We couldn't see one. There was only the group in the draining pen, the holding pen was quite empty.

'Where is it then?' asked Janet.

Daniel had decided it was fun time.

Rabbits On Report

'It's this old ram here,' said David, charging towards me. Suddenly there was sixteen stones of power heading my way. Seated as I was on the top rail of a five-bar fence I didn't stand a cat in hell's chance of getting away. It appeared Daniel was about to settle a few old scores. He picked me off that fence like a sack of potatoes while the others cheered and laughed. I was on my way to the sheep dip. He held me over the murky brown water. Oh well, there was nothing I could do. If Daniel had decided I was going in the sheep dip,

Dipping Time

I was going in the sheep dip and none of the others was prepared to rescue me. All I could do was close my eyes, think of England and wait for that sinking feeling. He held me over the bath and I looked down at the 'gunge'. It didn't look at all inviting, in fact most unedifying.

'Shall I dip him?' he shouted and a loud chorus replied 'Yes' – even Janet who I thought might be on my side.

I was beginning to feel nervous. I thought, if he drops me in there I shall sink like a stone and come up smelling like a drain. It wasn't a very cheerful prospect because I wouldn't want to get in the car soaking wet with that stuff and spoil the upholstery, but I would be in desperate need of a shower and a change of clothes. I was also worried it might be detrimental to my health.

Daniel then started to liven things up a bit by lowering me down so my backside was almost touching the water. I thought, 'if his back gives way now I'm a gonner.' Then he took me right back up away from it. My relief was short lived however, when I found myself back within a few inches of the surface. Everyone, except me, was very excited now and it was just like a pantomime with Daniel shouting 'Oh no I won't' and everyone replying, 'Oh yes you will.'

'I'll save you this time,' said Daniel graciously and put me back on my feet. But was my face red? I suppose I felt a little embarrassed in front of them all but there you go, you have to take the rough with the smooth. I was well aware that come Monday morning the whole staff room would be a-buzz with my latest escapade and there would be some well-thought out comments from my colleagues.

Fun time was over and it was back to work. We loaded the last of the sheep up. Three of my pupils came back with me to unload them at David's farm. The ewes were back together with their lambs again and at last they were quiet. We all returned to school. Janet, Daniel and Susan stayed a while longer at the Finneys' farm to clean out the dipping tank and the concrete surround of the pens. Finally the cover was put back on the dipping tank to prevent anyone falling in. We all met back at the school, cleaned out the trailer and then it was lunch time. The temperature was up in the eighties. We all needed a bath and change of clothes. I thanked them all for their help and hard work and told them to enjoy the rest of the weekend. They deserved it. The pupils cycled off home and Janet gave Daniel a lift back. It had been another good day.

Chapter Seven
A New Heifer Arrives

When Eleanor wrote to the Queen telling her about Crystal I told my pupils not to expect an early reply. Her Majesty had far more important things to attend to than a school in the Midlands but to everyone's surprise and delight we got a reply from Buckingham Palace within ten days. A letter arrived addressed, not to me but to Miss Eleanor Wallis. There was no stamp on it, just a mauve circle with a crown and E II R inside the circle plus a first-class mark. On the back of the envelope was the family's red coat of arms.

When Eleanor collected the letter from me she could hardly contain her excitement but, fair play to her, she didn't open it straight away but saved it until break time when she could open it in front of all the other farm helpers. I warned her not to be too disappointed as I couldn't really see the Queen letting us have another heifer.

Everyone was on edge waiting for the result and we were relieved to hear it was good news. It said that the farm manager at Windsor had been contacted, a new heifer had been chosen for us and we were to visit the Royal Farms to collect her as soon as possible. As the heifer's name was Windsor Grand Good News this letter really did convey 'good news'. The letter also said that the Queen was looking forward to reading my book 'Ducks In Detention', which Eleanor had sent her.

There were whoops and cheers of joy and I got a bit nervous in case the headmaster heard the goings on and came to see what it was all about. I immediately telephoned the farm manager who informed me that Good News was a fabulous heifer, of show quality, had the potential to produce a vast amount of good-quality milk and was just one year old. This Jersey heifer with a pedigree longer than mine could be ours for just £250. He also said that we were not paying the full price, but because we were a school we were looked on very favourably. After talking to the farm manager I then had to telephone the farm herdsman, Trevor

Burwood. I had dealt with him before when we had bought Crystal, our first Royal Jersey.

I had free periods for the whole of Wednesday afternoon so I asked if I could visit the very next Wednesday. By choosing that day I didn't have to worry about other staff covering my lessons. I arranged with Trevor to be at the Royal Farms at 2.30pm.

I did all this without checking if the school minibus was free. Fortunately it was so I could take more students than if I travelled in my car.

After school I gathered all my helpers around and told them of the arrangements. They were all excited and naturally everyone wanted the afternoon off to visit Windsor and fetch the new heifer.

It's not a quick job organising half- a-dozen pupils to have time off. Firstly I needed permission off Mr Beech. Then I had to decide which pupils to take – I couldn't take them all. Obviously Eleanor would go because she had instigated the whole affair. She had composed and written the letter to Buckingham Palace in the first place. Jason, Louise, Jonathon, Michael and Angela were the others chosen. The next step was to get written permission from their parents and the final hurdle was to get permission from their teachers to miss their lessons. Some staff, like Miss Perrin, were only too pleased to let the students go while others, like Mr Harris would definitely say 'no' just to be awkward.

After a bit of wheedling I got the go ahead. I didn't sleep very well at all on the Tuesday night before the visit. I had studied the road map, it was fairly easy and I had been before. It was the M1 for most of the way then the M25 and then a fairly short drive around Windsor but I still kept dreaming that we got stuck on the M25 and just kept driving round and round and round.

Wednesday morning seemed to fly by. I had written each of the students a note for the dinner ladies so they could be first in to school lunch. I was actually the first in to the school canteen. I had let my pupils go dead on time – not a minute before because if Mr Beech saw them out early it was a hanging offence.

A New Heifer Arrives

I was closely followed into lunch by the chosen six. They all joined me at the same table. They had all chosen chips (what else?), some with burgers, some with fish and all of them had baked beans. I took a deep breath and let out a sigh as I suspected this was going to be a very musical afternoon with a high-octane aroma.

The food was disappearing at a great rate of knots because they were all eager to get on the road but there were two, Jason and Jonathon, who could eat quickly, carry on a conversation and a comedy double act all at the same time.

'This meal's a lot different to the one I had last evening,' Jason remarked seriously.

'Really? Why's that?' asked Angela.

'I went out for a slap-up meal with my mum and dad, it was my mum's birthday – it was fabulous. I had prawn cocktail for starters followed by duck in orange sauce and a gateau for sweet. We had wine and lots more to drink besides.'

'It must have cost a fortune,' said Eleanor.

'Where did you go?' asked Jonathon.

'Oh to the Swan, don't you know,' Jason replied in an upper-crust accent.

'You keep talking like that and you'll be right at home with the Royals,' I said.

'We couldn't afford to go the the Swan,' said Jonathon with a straight face. 'We go for a pub lunch sometimes in the Black Boar - it is really downmarket. I bet you go there all the time don't you, sir?' he added.

'No I don't,' I snapped.

'It is so common ...'

Right, here comes the cabaret, I thought.

'You can have a chop for £2.50 but if you have a chop with lamb on it it's £5. New potatoes are only 75p but second hand ones are only 50p and you get a choice of table cloth, either the "Sun" or the "Mirror".'

He scooped another large helping of beans into his mouth and carried on talking: 'There's a sign in the window which says customers who pay for food and then sneak out without eating it will be prosecuted.'

'I don't get that,' said Angela, looking bewildered.

'I'll explain it,' offered Jonathon.

'Look, explain later – I've finished my meal and so has everyone else. We're waiting for you Jonathon, come on hurry up.' I was ready to go.

'Come on, we want to get away,' said Louise impatiently.

'Yes, come on, get it down you and stop yapping,' said Michael.

'Every time a sheep baas it loses a mouthful,' I said wisely.

The action of fork from plate to mouth and back again was like a mechanical digger and we watched with fascination as this piece of precision engineering cleared every last morsel.

At last everyone was finished. We collected the minibus and hitched up the trailer. They had all brought drinks, sandwiches, crisps, chocolate bars, apples and lots more besides so if we had the misfortune to be besieged by pirates, highwaymen or any other such villains we could hold out for days. A quick visit to what our cousins across the pond call 'the bathroom' and we were all ready to go.

'Do you know the way, sir?' asked Eleanor.

'Yes, I've been before and I studied the map last night as well,' I replied, trying to appear confident.

'We should have brought my mum, sir,' said Jason loudly.

'Don't shout,' said Eleanor sternly.

'What's your mum got to do with it?' asked Michael.

'She's got varicose veins and my dad says if they get any worse he can use her legs as a road map.'

'That's not very nice,' I said but secretly I was smiling. We were all in great spirits.

The traffic was not too heavy and we made good time to Windsor. I had to consult my map but once on the right road we soon found the large gates to the Royal Farms. I knew what to expect after my last visit. A gatekeeper in a smart green uniform checked my name and minibus number plates as we were on a list of visitors. The gate was opened and we drove in. A long, private drive with well-kept fields on either side stretched before us. We drove along and as we got closer to the farm buildings we could see some of the

A New Heifer Arrives

pedigree Jersey cows looking out of a covered yard, somewhere amongst all those cattle was one who would be returning to school with us.

'This looks really, really smart,' remarked Angela.

'Well what do you expect? The Queen owns it all,' answered Louise.

Jonathon immediately went into his Prince Charles routine. Then I joined in.

'We might see him,' said Michael optimistically.

'No chance,' I said.

As always the Royal Farms looked immaculate with old farm buildings and new modern cattle yards blending in together and as ever, neat and tidy. The pupils were pretty good at keeping the school farm clean and clutter free but I thought a little reminder wouldn't do any harm.

'Right all of you, just note how tidy everywhere is, no rake left lying about, no shovels propping up the walls, look, learn and inwardly digest.'

Howls of protest came from behind me.

'Oh come on, sir, that's not fair.' And 'For crying out loud I only straightened that tool shed out last week.' And so on.

We pulled up in the farmyard. There was no straw lying around nor anything for anyone to slip, trip or fall over.

'See what I mean?' I said. There were no replies this time, they were all in awe of the place.

Trevor Burwood, the stockman, came out of one of the cattle yards, strode over to the minibus and shook hands with me.

'You're right on time. It's exactly 3.30pm,' he said.

'If Mr Terry says he'll be here at 3.30pm then 3.30pm it is. Not 3.25pm or 3.35pm,' said Jonathon.

'This is Jonathon,' I said and then introduced all the others. I told them that Trevor had been very good on advising us on the pedigree Jerseys over the years, for instance when we had our first Royal calf, Windsor Coronets Crystal 6th.

Trevor asked us how long we could stay and I told him we had plenty of time. I also told him the students had brought plenty of provisions including 'pop' and crisps.

'Goodness, are you stocking up for a siege?' he laughed. 'While you're here I'd like to show you the cows first then I'll show you the heifer that you hope to purchase.'

The 130 cows were housed in cubicles and covered yards. My students had never seen such a wonderful herd and I could tell by their faces they were most impressed. Trevor told them that the herd was started up in Queen Victoria's reign.

'Do you know when that was?' he asked.

'Yes sir,' said Angela quickly. 'It was from 1837 to 1901.'

'Well done,' said Trevor, 'Well now, many of the cows bred on the farm have been exported to many other countries. We have supplied cattle to the Middle East, Africa and Canada.'

'How big is the farm?' asked Eleanor.

'Tell me how big your school farm is first,' Trevor said.

'Our school farm is one acre,' replied Eleanor proudly 'or 0.405 hectares.'

'The Queen's farm is about 2,000 acres or 800 hectares. It covers about twelve miles by six miles.'

The looks of amazement on my pupil's faces were a sight to behold.

'The farm buildings wouldn't fit on the whole of our farm,' remarked Jonathon. He was probably right. Trevor explained that as well as the Jersey cows they also grew winter wheat, winter barley, rape and beans, and had a herd of pedigree Ayrshire cattle as well as pigs and turkeys.

We were shown the milking parlour and the old dairy designed and created by Prince Albert and still in use to this day. It had wonderful marble-topped tables and exotically tiled cavity walls which were no less than four feet thick. Its stained glass windows made a very grand and unusual building and with all that marble and tiles it was beautifully cool. Some of the Jersey milk in this dairy was used to make cream and cream cheese for the Royal family.

We were then shown a covered cattle yard which was full of young heifers. Trevor went into the yard and the cattle moved around him.

'That's her.' He pointed to what seemed to be the best-looking animal in the yard. She positively glowed. She was

A New Heifer Arrives

fawn in colour with a white patch on her shoulder and for one year old she was very well grown indeed.

'She looks fabulous,' gasped Eleanor.

We looked at her for a few minutes, with everyone stretching out to touch her.

'We agreed the price of £250 on the telephone and that's what it stands at, there's no bartering to do so would you like her?' Trevor asked.

'As if we could say no. Of course we'd like her wouldn't we? Hands up those who would like to take her with us back to school.' Every hand shot in the air and looking at their radiant faces and shining eyes I couldn't have said no even if I had wanted to. We had bought our second Royal heifer.

'She is very well bred indeed,' said Trevor. He went on to say that her sire was a famous New Zealand bull called Ferdon Grand Glory and her dam was called Windsor Tandras Black Magic, an excellent three-year-old cow bred on the Royal Farms.

'Black Magic's mother is called Windsor Lionhearts Good News and her grandmother is called Windsor Coronets Good News 3rd. I can't remember any further back without looking up the pedigrees,' Trevor said.

'You've done very well to remember all that lot,' I said. 'I did notice one thing, perhaps my students have noticed as well.' Before I could say more Eleanor came back with: 'I've got it. This new heifer Windsor Grand Good News – well, her grandmother Windsor Coronets Good News 3rd is related to our very first heifer which we bought from here, Windsor Coronets Crystal 6th – Coronets is the clue,' she said triumphantly.

'That's quite right, very good. Your original heifer was Windsor Coronets Crystal 6th. Their shared relation is the bull Ferdon Glens Coronet.'

Louise was scratching her head and looking puzzled. 'It's very complicated,' she said.

'I wish my pedigree was half as good,' said Jonathon.

'All of this here today is a different world, here we are on a farm twelve miles long by six miles wide owned by the Queen, we're surrounded by some of the best cattle in the world, I don't know, it really is a long, long way from the small terraced house I live in,' said Louise.

'It's a known fact that two-thirds of the world don't know how the other half lives,' said Jonathon.

I looked at him, was he joking or just bad at sums?

'Who is your maths teacher?' Jason asked.

'Mr Martin,' came the prompt reply and we all laughed because he did seem blissfully unaware of his comical blunder.

'Are you sure you want this heifer?' asked Trevor again.

'Oh yes, yes, yes please, we would love to take her back with us.'

Trevor led the way to the farm office. On the way we stopped off at the cows again and he pointed out Good News's mother and grandmother – they were both fine-looking animals. While in the office Trevor gave us the heifer's registration certificate. This was our second animal to have the coveted ear tattoo HM. Her correct number was HM T39.

'So all we've got to do now is load her up into the trailer, and then pay you, of course,' I said politely.

Trevor fetched a halter from one of the barns and a bucket which was half-filled with cattle cake, a titbit no self-respecting cow or heifer can resist. He entered the yard and was immediately surrounded by greedy cattle. They certainly knew what the bucket contained. We could hardly see him for golden-coloured bodies. He was watching Good News out of the corner of his eye and we could easily spot her. Like all her kith and kin she became very interested in the bucket. She plunged her nose in, liked the smell of whatever was in there and was soon eating the cattle cake very quickly. While she was busy enjoying herself Trevor slipped the halter on to the top of her head, moved the bucket away and then slipped the halter under her chin. The second it was in place she was well and truly caught. Eleanor then went into the yard to help. She took the bucket and shook it in front of Good News. The heifer followed it like a donkey following a carrot. I opened the back of the trailer ready to get her inside. It was well bedded down with clean straw so she would be quite comfortable on the journey – the greedy little madam just

A New Heifer Arrives

followed the bucket into the trailer and hey presto she was all loaded up ready to go to her new home. Trevor removed the halter and slipped out of the side door of the trailer.

We then had to trail all the way back to the office – following Trevor like the pied piper of Hamelin – to finish the formalities. I wrote out the cheque to 'The Royal Farms' for the agreed price. No bartering – I didn't want to end up in the Tower – and the deal was swiftly done.

Trevor then spoke to the students. 'Before you go I must explain to you all the feeding instructions, in fact, I'll give you a bag of food to take with you so that you can introduce your ration gradually. Too drastic a change too quickly could result in you having a very sick little heifer on your hands and none of us wants that do we?'

The students were giving him their full attention so didn't notice the farm manager accompanied by another person coming into view. The newcomer was a smartly dressed fellow in a suit to die for and a pair of green wellingtons. He looked familiar and I started to wonder where I had seen him before. He had a red face, from being in the open air a lot I supposed, and rather large ears which stuck out. It was a minute or two before the penny dropped and I realised it was Prince Charles. I knew Trevor had noticed him but he still carried on talking to us. The two men were getting nearer and I could see at this point that His Royal Highness had his arm in a sling and could hear what they were saying.

Then I could hear their conversation clearly. The farm manager was saying 'I read about it in the newspapers, sir, and there was a news bulletin on the television. But if you don't mind me asking – what really happened to your arm?' he asked.

'I was on my polo pony, having a rather good chukka when the wretched animal threw me off. I landed heavily on this arm and I was rushed off the nearest hospital at Cirencester which is actually a National Health hospital.'

'Did you receive good treatment, sir?'

'Yes, within about twenty minutes of me arriving the chairman of the Gloucestershire Health Authority came out to meet me.'

'I hope he was pleasant and helpful.'

'Indeed he was. He said it was the first time a king had been admitted to their hospital. I told him "I'm not the King" and he said you probably will be by the time we get round to treating you what with all the health cuts and waiting lists.' And the pair of them roared with laughter.

I turned my attentions back to Trevor and his talk about feeding the cattle but Prince Charles's conversation was much more interesting and I found myself eavesdropping again. The prince was describing, in graphic detail, the operation on his arm. 'Finally' he said 'they took some skin from here' – he pointed to his rear – 'and grafted it on to here,' – he pointed to his elbow.'

'Well, you have been "through the mill" sir. How are you feeling now?'

'What? Apart from not knowing my arse from my elbow?' Again the two of them roared with laughter.

It was time for us to leave. We thanked Trevor again and set off for home. We hadn't been on the road long before Angela asked 'Was that Prince Charles in the yard?'

'Yes it was,' I replied.

'Ah. I thought it was, and I saw you earwigging.'

'Oh no you didn't,' I protested.

'Oh yes we did,' they chorused.

We were making good time on the M1 when suddenly I noticed steam coming out from under the bonnet. I pulled over on to the hard shoulder. There was a good-sized grassy bank nearby so for safety reasons I got my students to clamber up it and over the top to the other side, well away from the traffic. I lifted the bonnet to try and ascertain the problem. The water in the radiator was obviously boiling and I had to wait for what seemed like ages for it to cool down. While I waited it dawned on me that I needed some water. I joined my students in the safety of their eyrie.

'I need some water for the radiator,' I said.

'I could do with going to the toilet,' said Jason.

'No thank you. I don't want that,' I said quickly.

'I still have some Malvern water left in my bottle,' said Angela helpfully.

'No, it's a shame to waste that in a radiator, you drink it. I can see a pond in that field,' I said.

'Where?' asked Angela, scanning the landscape.

'Well, I can't actually see a pond but I can see a circle of willow trees so it follows there must be a pond there.'

'We need something to carry it in,' said Louise.

'I'll drink my Malvern water and you can have that for one bottle, sir,' offered Angela.

Deep rooting about in bags produced two more water bottles and two 'pop' bottles. I sent Michael and Jonathon off to fill them. I just hoped they really would bring pond water back, after Jason's offer – well – who knew what they might come back with?

'Be careful,' I called after them. 'You could be trespassing on someone's property and the last thing I want is some bad-tempered farmer having a go at us.'

The radiator was soon filled and then, erring on the side of caution, Michael and Jonathon went back again to refill the bottles so we would have a reserve supply.

We set off again and I watched the water temperature gauge this time – I hadn't even noticed it before. Twenty minutes into the resumed journey and it was slowly creeping up into the red, it was obvious the water was going to boil again.

'Well, I could do with a cup of tea, anybody got any tea bags? We could have a brew,' said Jason, trying to cheer us all up.

'Be quiet,' said Louise but luck was on our side as a sign post saying 'Services' came into view. I drove the minibus into the car park and everyone got out. The students checked Good News in her trailer and found her to be fine.

Water was dripping our of the radiator and leaving a puddle on the car park – wonderful – we had a leak somewhere and obviously the small amount of water that was left in the tank was getting too hot.

We made good use of the services. Jason got his cup of tea, the others all telephoned home to let their parents know we would be late and we used the wash basins in the toilets to fill up the bottles again. The radiator took seven bottles of water this time. We even sorted through the rubbish bins to try and find some more empty bottles to fill in reserve for the rest of the journey.

'Couldn't we get the RAC out, sir?' asked Michael.

'We could, we are members but with the trailer and Good News it could be a bit of a problem. I don't know if they would put the trailer on the transporter – I can't imagine they would be too keen.'

I decided to try and drive home – even if it took another two or three stops. In actual fact it took only one more before we got home.

A New Heifer Arrives

We arrived back at school nearly two hours later than planned. The students that hadn't been with us had fed the animals so it was just a matter of quickly unloading Good News. We gave her some hay and water and bedded her down in clean straw.

'Are you sure she will be all right on her own?' asked Michael.

'Yes, she'll be fine, don't worry,' I said confidently. 'Everybody go home now and we can fuss over her in the morning.' I was dog-tired and wanted to get home myself. It wasn't long before I was in bed sleeping like a log.

Next morning I parked my car on the staff car park as normal but that's about all that was normal. Good News was in full song, kicking up such a noise pupils were gathered in groups wondering what on earth was going on. She was mooing and mooing and mooing at too many decibels for comfort.

Before I could open the door to her building one of our neighbours, a Mrs Clarke, leaned over the garden hedge.

'I'm fed up with that bloody racket. What are you going to do about it?' Pleasantries were conspicuous by their absence.

'Hold on a minute Mrs Clarke. I've only just got here and heard her,' I replied.

'Well you're bloody lucky, we've had to listen to it all night. My Reginald and myself have had no sleep at all and I mean no sleep, not a wink, she hasn't stopped mooing all damn night.'

'I am sorry, I had no idea she would kick up like this. I'll just check on her and see if I can find what the problem is.'

By this time my helpers were beginning to arrive and didn't bother to hide their amusement because I was being told off.

'Why is she mooing like that, sir?' I was asked.

'How the devil do I know, I've only just got here myself.' I snapped.

I had a look at her. She hadn't touched her hay or water. Something was definitely wrong with our Royal newcomer.

She went quiet – it was bliss. I got in with her, she was walking all right, her eyes were bright, her nose was fine, no diarrhoea, there didn't appear to be anything wrong.

Heifers and cows, when they are on heat or bulling, as it is called, will moo a lot but Trevor had told me that she was bulling less than one week ago so it wasn't that.

'What's the matter with her, sir?' asked Angela pitifully.

'Come on sir, you're the expert. What's up with her?' asked Jonathon.

'Of course,' I said in a flash of inspiration, 'She's lonely. She's on her own, left all her sisters and companions behind, she needs a friend.'

'But we haven't got any more cattle at the moment,' said Angela.

'We all know that,' retorted Louise.

'Perhaps the school Theatrical Society will lend you their cow, sir,' remarked Jonathon in a cheeky voice. 'You could be the back end, Mr Terry, and Mr Beech could be the front.'

Mrs Clarke was shouting again. Another neighbour, Mrs West, joined her and the two of them had a real go at me. I had a heifer with a friendless complex vocalising like a prima donna and two irate housewives giving me an ear bending and it was only 9.15am. What a day I had in prospect.

I needed another heifer and pretty soon. I hadn't got the time to buy or borrow one and the headmaster's assembly time was looming large on the horizon. I dared not miss as it was another hanging offence.

I waited until after Mr Beech's Assembly – which of course was interrupted about twenty-five times by Good News mooing. I needed to tell him we had bought a new heifer, although I think he was well aware of that fact by now. I also had to inform him that the minibus was about to expire because of a leaky radiator and that I needed another heifer, preferably within the next half hour.

'Mr Beech, can I have a word please?' I asked.

'No time now Mr Terry. I have a parent waiting to see me. After school if you don't mind.' He walked off but he did turn round briefly to say, 'Shut that damn animal up will you – please.'

I went up to the staff room and telephoned Dennis Hayes, a cattle dealer and slaughterman. It was he who had the job of putting Crystal down. I told him my problem. Again luck was with me because he told me he had a small Aberdeen Angus cross Holstein-Friesian heifer to sell. She was just ten months old and the price was £100. I hadn't got time to barter.

'I'll take her,' I said.

Dennis agreed to bring her to the school as soon as possible.

'Look Dennis, make it quick will you or I'm going to be invited to a lynching party and I'm the party that's going to be lynched.'

I was late for the first lesson of the day – yet another hanging offence. To keep Good News company and quieten her down I took the pupils along to see her. It was exactly what she wanted, company. While we were there she was fine but as soon as we left the mooing started again.

At break time I was relieved to see Dennis Hayes drive his cattle truck around to the school farm. He unloaded a lovely little black heifer. We put her in with Good News. They sniffed each other, obviously liked each other and we had silence. It was wonderful.

Chapter Eight
National Curriculum

Was it the news of the day? Or the news of the month? Neither, it was the news of the year. The Government was about to introduce a thing called the National Curriculum into every state school in the country.

The powers that be in Westminster, including the education department, had decreed that this was just what the country needed.

That evening I watched the television news and listened as the newsreader said that all state schools in England and Wales would be taught the same subject syllabuses. They would start with three core subjects: mathematics, English and science. Other subjects of geography, history, modern languages, art, music, PE, RE, technology and information technology would be introduced at a later date.

The 'Times Education Supplement' was full of it. There would still be different examination boards and the syllabus issued from the different boards would differ slightly but basically, all schools would be doing the same courses with the same attainment targets and common assessment levels.

Up until then not all students received the same education. Schools could differ from county to county, even from town to town. The National Curriculum would put a stop to all that and subjects would be standardised across the country.

As the weeks turned into months the paperwork started to appear in schools and as time went by it became glaringly obvious to me that the subject of rural studies was not getting a mention. I was the first to acknowledge that not all schools could cater for the subject because not all schools had a garden and far fewer schools had the facilities to keep small livestock, let alone the larger animals like cattle, sheep, pigs and goats. Also there would not be enough specialist rural studies teachers to go round and, of course not all schools would want to teach the subject anyway. I came to the reluctant conclusion that this National Curriculum did not look good for rural studies, my students nor of course, myself.

For subjects such as mathematics and English it would be ideal educationally because students living, for example, in Devon, would be taught the same subjects and subject content as students living in Warwickshire or as far away as Tyne and Wear and no particular area would be at a disadvantage due to a poor curriculum.

Over the weeks, more information poured in and the number of hours for each subject taught per week was calculated. Still rural studies was omitted.

All this worry came on top of teaching a full timetable, the school farm and gardens, animals to feed, plants to water, parents' evenings to attend, homework and exam papers to mark. Anyone who thinks a teacher's life is an easy option should try it.

I told myself that surely we would be allowed to keep rural studies at our school. I had built up a fantastic department from sticks and stones and a mud patch. It was my empire and it had brought prestige to the school with a show flock winning all the time. There had been one season when I had thrown down the gauntlet to my farming friends by saying we would win a hundred prizes. It was quite a challenge but believe it or not we did it. How could the education minister ignore such achievements and just throw all that out of the window? I hoped there would be some leeway whereby we could keep our department up and running but in the meantime it was I who was running – on my energy reserves and all the time the weeks were flying by.

One Thursday morning, ten minutes into my first lesson, one of my older students, Mark, arrived late.

'Oh good morning,' I said sarcastically. 'Nice of you to join us, is there anything we can get you? Tea perhaps, or some lightly charred toast? Where the devil have you been? Up Snog Alley I suppose,' I said sternly, naming the students' colloquialism for the back of the bike sheds.

'Sorry I'm late Mr Terry. Mr Beech asked me into his office,' he explained, gasping for breath.

'Oh and what have you done this time?' I asked.

National Curriculum

'Nothing.'

'Well, of course you haven't! Mr Beech doesn't ask you into his office for nothing so what have you been up to?'

'Well, if you must know, sir, he caught me and my girlfriend kissing and cuddling in the playground and to be honest, sir, my hands were everywhere.'

I could hear the muffled sniggers of the rest of the class and I tried my best to keep a straight face.

'And what did Mr Beech say to that?'

'He told me not to be so stupid using the playground and to use a bit of common in the future but I don't know any common near here.'

At this the class erupted and I had to turn my back and make a great show of cleaning the blackboard to hide my own amusement. I couldn't help myself.

Soon after it was my turn to be invited into the inner sanctum.

'Well, Mr Terry, the writing is on the wall,' he stated as I entered.

'Yes I know I've seen it. Some idiot has written "Dyslexia Rules K.O." on the front of the school,' I replied.

'No, no, no. I don't mean it like that, I'm talking about your subject, rural studies. The National Curriculum has dropped it and it means that very shortly it will be a dead subject, it will disappear from the curriculum in just about all state schools including this one.'

'It can't,' I cried in alarm.

'It can and it most definitely will.'

'Oh, not this school?'

'Yes Mr Terry, this school.'

'But surely we can keep it up and running – just look at the benefits it has given to the students over the years, and the glory it has brought to the school' I argued, trying to appeal to his vanity.

'It's none of my doing. National Curriculum dictates the number of hours per week for each subject, not me, and from what I can see there will be no time left over,' he replied.

'But without rural studies our students know so very little about the countryside and its wildlife. They're "townies".' I argued my case but deep down I thought I was wasting my breath and my time. But I wasn't going down without a fight.

After this little chat I immediately started writing letters to anyone I could think of who might take an interest in our cause including the chairman of governors, my MP and even the education secretary in London.

I wrote to other rural studies teachers and on the whole it looked pretty hopeless. It looked as if a few schools would retain the subject but ours was not among them. To all intents and purposes the school had one rural studies teacher, one garden and a selection of farm animals surplus to requirements.

The first action to be implemented was to take rural studies off the timetable in the upper school and in its place I had to teach some lower school science but at least while rural studies remained in the lower school there was a glimmer of hope that someone in the upper echelons of power would have a change of heart.

Finally I was called to Mr Beech's office. The die was cast. I was informed that rural studies had been taken off the timetable completely. I was shattered, I felt like a deflated balloon. I was then given a choice, albeit Hobson's choice. I was offered a job as a full-time science teacher, teaching combined science in the lower school and biology in the upper school. It was either that or find another career. As I said, it was Hobson's choice.

One bright light did manage to pierce the gloom. Although official funding for the farm would stop because it was no longer a National Curriculum subject I could keep it on myself for educational purposes to use before and after school and during the holidays and it could also be used for science and biology lessons. Perhaps other staff would like to use it for teaching other subjects, in particular, art.

I had only partly won the battle but at least the war wasn't lost – yet. The farm and garden would stay but formal tuition in rural studies would cease and I would have to adjust to teaching science.

Up until then I had been a 'one-man band' – a head of department with just one or two staff teaching just a few lessons of rural studies per week. My timetable was full, even though it was the only subject I taught.

My mobile classroom was set away from the rest of the school, I had an acre of land, the farm and the garden. I was extremely busy, I had a syllabus to follow, but for most of the time I was my own boss. Mr Beech just let me carry on with my work. If I wanted to teach students to trim sheep's feet on a Monday morning and how to prune roses on a Wednesday afternoon then I did it – I didn't have to ask anyone's permission. I had books to mark, examinations and tests to prepare and I even wrote a CSE examination paper. There were parents evenings but life was good – I rarely had Mr Beech looking over my shoulder. Unfortunately all that was about to change.

I was quite engrossed in my daydreaming when I suddenly became aware that one of the students, Glen, was squinting over his book.

'What's the matter Glen, can't you see the print properly?' I asked.

'No sir, I've lost my glasses and I'm hopeless without them.'

'Where did you have them last?' I asked.

'I can't remember, sir, and I can't look for them until I find them,' he replied.

I couldn't argue. How do you argue with a catch-22 situation?

'You've got brilliant eyesight sir, not much gets past you does it?' said Sarah.

'No. I don't miss a trick,' I said modestly.

'Have you ever had your eyes checked?' she asked.

'No' I said 'they've always been brown' – a remark met with a chorus of catcalls, boos and whistles.

'My grandfather is ninety-one and he has never needed glasses,' Robert stated proudly.

'Well, good for him,' I replied.

'No sir, he always drinks straight from the bottle,' he said and chortled at his own cleverness. Teacher had again walked straight into their little trap. Things would change a lot when I became a science teacher and a member of a team.

I would teach a combined science course in the lower school. I would get the same class for four lessons a week and I would have to teach them biology, chemistry and physics. Topics and projects would include practical experiments, some to be shown as demonstration experiments with other experiments to be completed by the students.

It had been a number of years since I had made the acquaintance of chemistry and physics. Actually it was when I was a pupil at school myself so I had a lot of catching up to do. I would have to set myself some homework.

In the upper school the subject was still called science but each group had three science teachers, a biology specialist, a physics specialist and a chemistry specialist. I would be a biology specialist taking each group for three lessons a week.

There would be top groups and mixed ability groups in all years and some of the work in all years would be investigative experiments. I would have to set the students a task and they had to plan it, carry it out and conclude it for themselves. This could possibly result in us waving goodbye to the roof. I had no worries about the biology experiments but the chemistry and physics cost me some sleep. I would have my work cut out keeping the odd one or two students out of trouble. I would also have to set more homework and as a member of a team I would be monitored myself.

The saddest thing of all was that my knowledge of environmental studies, agriculture and horticulture would now be put on the back burner and not passed on during lesson time. There was a small amount of environmental studies in the science classes and a very tiny bit of agriculture but no horticulture. These small proportions were for 'townies'. I had all the wonderful facilities to teach down-to-earth countryside skills like milking goats, lambing, planting and growing vegetables and much, much more and it was going to waste. Didn't those high-ups in their ivory towers realise that some town children love learning about nature? Where are the future David Attenboroughs and other animal experts coming from if not from our schools? It really grated on my nerves that I had spent my life building up this rural studies department and for seventeen years of my career I never took a day's holiday. As well as my life it was my hobby. I was so angry and frustrated.

If I wasn't going to receive any funding for the farm I would have to hone and polish my old, almost forgotten skills as a scrounger and become even more proficient at it. In the old days, when we were building up the department I could scrounge fleas off a dog. Now it looked as if I would have to do it again because there was no way I was going to let the farm and garden go. I was on a crusade. Mr Beech said that if the farm couldn't keep going financially and began to lose money the school would not help out and the farm and gardens would have to close.

It was imperative I kept the farm on an even keel. I felt I owed it to all those students that had worked on and benefited from the farm in the past and I also owed it to my present students and the ones that hadn't yet started at the school.

Chapter Nine
Keeping The School Farm Up And Running

Our new heifer Windsor Grand Good News was being fed on a really good, palatable diet but we didn't give her too much. It wouldn't do her any favours to get her over fat.

We fed her on what is called 'Coarse Mix' – a cattle feed mixture containing cattle cake, linseed cake, barley, dried peas, locust beans and molasses. It's so good and sweet that in the past students have picked the locust beans out and ate them themselves. These days, of course, the practice is frowned upon because of the many food poisoning cases we seem to get.

The Royal Farms had given us a bag of coarse mix and I bought more of the same brand. The firm that I bought it from, Dalimores, did not supply our other animal feeds which were supplied by Peters Feeds. This started me wondering about sponsorship.

I telephoned Dalimores and told the girl on reception that I really needed to speak to the manager. I was put through to Mr John Roberts and I told him all our problems. He said he would think things over and chat with his sales representative, a Mr Bill Jones.

A few days later they telephoned and arranged to see me after school had finished on a Monday evening. They were keen to get the school's custom and they gave me a bag of coarse mix feed there and then free of charge.

'I want you to stop having cattle, sheep, pig and poultry feed from your usual suppliers and transfer to our firm,' said Mr Roberts.

He was very interested in our sheep and I could see his mind working overtime. The school got a lot of publicity and that could mean publicity for his firm.

'Well, we've talked it through and to sponsor you we will give you one bag of coarse ration for every show you attend,' he said.

'That's sounds quite generous,' I said. 'But is there a catch?'

'No catch as long as you and your students put up a sign

at the shows saying the livestock is fed on our foodstuffs.'

'I'll have to think it over,' I said, 'as I am quite pleased with the food I get from Peters.'

'Maybe, but Peters aren't giving you anything are they John?'

'No,' I replied but thought to myself, they might even offer more than Dalimores.

'I won't make a decision now,' I added. I knew it would pay me to wait and speak to Peters Feeds.

Before these two gentlemen left my classroom I decided to do a bit of sales pitching myself and offered them everything from eggs to a potted plant. As they staggered out loaded with produce from the school farm, one of my teaching colleagues was heard to mutter, 'That John Terry, he could sell lawn mowers to tower block tenants.'

The school farm was still viable and it was comments like that that made me realise we were on the right track. I was pleased. It was almost true. I had once seriously thought about becoming a salesman – an agricultural salesman. I've certainly got the 'gift of the gab' and I reckoned I would like the life, even though some salesmen are regarded, with some justification, as a darned nuisance but they are a necessary evil and only doing their job.

Some have the knack of arriving at a farm just when the farmer is having a well-earned lunch or working flat out to get the harvesting finished, or racing against time to get bales of dry straw into a barn before the weather breaks.

Many farmers in our area have fought back with signs at the gate reading 'Sales reps by appointment only'. The dedicated rep then blithely ignores these signs. He drives right up to the farmhouse to be greeted with, 'What the hell are you doing here? Can't you read?' The stock reply to this polite enquiry is usually 'Yes sir. I've just come to make an appointment.'

Having got the proverbial foot in the door his real pitch is not long in coming.

'While I'm here sir, I wonder if you have tried our new product? Let me demonstrate' and before the farmer can bat an eyelid he's bought whatever the product is there and then because it's just too much damn trouble to go back into the house to find his diary and make the appointment.

When I first started to develop the school farm we never saw a farm sales rep, which I suppose is just as well because we hadn't got money to splash around buying off some fast-talking 'Del Boy' Trotter of the farming world and they probably thought it was not worth their while to call at some 'glorified allotment'.

To be fair to the salesmen, at that stage we were not well known and most reps would not have heard of us. As the years passed, however, and our achievements at shows brought lots of publicity we became a prime target.

There are good reps and bad reps and I soon discovered how to identify the good ones. They are the ones who have done the 'homework' and can talk one to one with the farmer before setting foot on his land.

The visit of John Roberts and Bill Jones certainly gave me something to think about as well as some ammunition to fire. I telephoned Peters and asked our usual rep, Tom Hendrick, to call. Tom didn't like to come second in life. I told him what the other firm had offered and that he might lose our custom if he couldn't better the offer.

'I'll do my best for you John. I can't make a better offer without checking with the manager back at the works but you can rely on me,' was his answer.

Two days later Tom brought the manager into the school. He was an official-looking person, tall and distinguished, wearing a dark grey suit, grey tie and carrying a leather briefcase. We sat at my desk and he came up with a firm offer of two bags of coarse concentrate ration at every show we attended and they would also supply our pupils with white coats with a small emblem and the title of their firm on the top pocket. This was a much better offer. I agreed. Unless the other firm gave me three bags of feed.

I then telephoned Dalimores and spoke to Bill Jones.

'We've been offered two bags of feed for every show we attend – you'll have to make it three if you want our custom,' I said boldly.

'I'd better check with John Roberts,' he said.

I waited patiently until he came back.

'I'm sorry Mr Terry, we can't manage three. I'm sorry we can't do business this time with you.'

I then rang Tom Hendrick back and I agreed to the deal. He came out to see me again the next day.

I had clinched my first sponsorship deal, a small deal but now I would do everything I could do to keep the school farm up and running.

Funny stories are part of the armoury of many salesmen and the true ones are often the funniest. I heard a corker from Tom Hendrick after he had left some free substitute calf milk and a thermometer with Mick, my old farm boss, whose unenlightened ways were something of a legend in the area. The thermometer was fixed to a flat rectangular piece of plastic with a small handle on top, the whole thing being about six inches long and two inches wide.

A week later the rep called to see how Mick was getting on with the milk.

'The milk is very good,' Mick said, 'but I couldn't get on with that damn thermometer – it was really hurting the poor calves.'

It transpired that Mick had not used the gadget for testing the milk. He had been taking the temperature of the calves with it and as you do not place a thermometer under a calf's tongue it was little wonder they were not very happy with the operation.

One week after my first sponsorship deal an ultra-keen salesman pulled up outside our classroom in a Ford Escort and bounced in all smiles and confidence.

'Good morning Mr Terry, how are you?'

'Very well, thank you,' I replied.

'You have a thriving school farm here,' he said. 'But I think I can improve things for you. Have you tried our popular animal foodstuffs?'

This chap didn't mess about. No beating around the bush with him. Get right in there. He wasn't going to waste time talking about my interests or his last holiday. Go for it – straight to the point. Before I could get a word in he said, 'You know these really are super foodstuffs, Mr Terry.'

Keeping The School Farm Up And Running

Now I'm not one to let the grass grow under my feet either and it was my turn to get a word in. 'Talking of foodstuffs,' I said with equal enthusiasm, 'we have some delicious home-grown foodstuffs here. Have you tried one of our apples? They are lovely and red and juicy. Better than any you can buy in the shops.' And as I spoke I pushed one into his hand.

'Well, they certainly look nice and juicy,' he said uncertainly. 'But you really must consider our foodstuffs' and still clutching the apple he soared into a world of his own expounding the virtues of his company's produce. He rattled on.

'I will sell you some of our pig food,' but before he could get any further I responded with 'Just one thing first – that will be seven pence for the apple.'

He gave in gracefully and took the money out of his pocket. After a lot more talk, mainly from him, he walked out of my classroom hugging his apple, two dozen eggs, a pint of goats milk, a cabbage and 5lb of potatoes.

As he climbed into his car I could see the bewildered look on his face. It seemed to say 'Hold on a minute! I'm the salesman, not him, so how come he's sold me all this lot and I haven't made a sale?'

I will give this rep full marks for perseverance. A week later he was back in the fray.

'You didn't fancy any of our pig feed Mr Terry,' he said. 'But what about calf feed? Now that's what you need. We have developed this marvellous new mix. It's very sweet and palatable, with sixteen percent protein and it's not expensive. Here is a sample. Come on – I'll persuade you this time, I'm the top salesman in our company and we cover the whole of the United Kingdom.'

I'm afraid to say he was wrong again. At the end of our discussion he left the classroom with a bag containing a dozen eggs, 5lb of carrots and 5lb of Brussels sprouts having again made no sale.

At his car he turned to me and said, 'How the devil do you do it? You're in the wrong bloody job, you ought to be running one of the large car factories such as Jaguar, they'd give their right arm to get a salesman like you, or you ought to be boss of a multinational industrial group. Come to think of it – why aren't you running the bloody country? I'm sure you could put it back on its feet.'

I never saw him again. A pity really, he was just what we needed to boost our farm funds.

In all modesty, I can say there is some truth in his assessment of my business acumen. In my job I have had to become a good businessman and now I had to become an even better one.

When I started to run the rural studies department in 1974 the County Council had given me a mere £100 to set up the operation. Even in those days that sort of money was a pittance. In my determination to build up a good department I was forced to become very 'tight' with the money I had.

Any money the department made was ploughed back in to buy things we needed, e.g. new feeding troughs, buckets, hayracks, paint and 101 other things. I never gave anything away.

With things looking gloomy financially I decided to start my lessons with a 'commercial' which went something along the lines of 'We have a great deal of farmyard manure to sell – it keeps piling up! It's already bagged up and we can deliver it in the trailer to your homes or your dad's allotment for twenty pence a bag. Oh yes, there will be a house point for every bag you sell.' At 20 pence a bag it almost flew out of the school.

In the autumn we sold fruit and vegetables, at Christmas time we were shouting the odds for turkeys, cockerels and pots of hyacinth bulbs. At the end of each term four pigs were slaughtered and eight customers sought to buy halves for their freezers. During the late summer we also sold a few lambs for the freezer.

An average of twelve oven-ready chickens were sold each week. In addition we had eggs and goats' milk to sell. In the climate created by the National Curriculum I would have to polish up my old skills and improve on them to sell the produce at an even greater rate.

Some 'townie' members of our staff raised their eyebrows at the 'For Sale' notices which kept appearing on the staff room notice board but they learned that I would sell anything if there was a profit in it. Mick, my old farm boss, used to say 'life is what you can get out of it – plus a little extra if you can find a few mugs.' I hope I'm note quite as bad as that but there was that time with the cauliflowers.

Twice a week I went to a local greengrocery to collect old cabbage leaves to feed to our livestock. The proprietor left them for me in boxes neatly stacked at the back of the shop. When I was collecting them one Tuesday lunchtime he came running out.

'Mr Terry. Wait a minute, I've got a dozen cauliflowers in the shop that have gone a bit yellow, would your sheep eat them?'

'They would love them,' I replied.

Back at the school I left the cauliflowers by the door of the classroom, intending to feed one or two of them to the sheep later on. While I was busy in the classroom Mr Bell, the deputy headmaster, happened to pass by.

'Oh I say, they look good cauliflowers. I expect you just picked them off the school vegetable garden. Look, I don't want to be greedy and do someone else out of them but the wife and I have just bought a new freezer. I'll buy the lot off you. I like to see your farm funds in good shape.'

'Fine' I said. 'I'll take thirty pence each for them.'

'Thank you Mr Terry. My wife will be delighted. You can't beat home-grown produce.'

I took the money, and no, I didn't run, I gave him the box of cauliflowers and wished him good afternoon. I shook my head in disbelief. There's one born every minute, I thought. He might have two degrees (one short of a pop group) but he certainly couldn't tell a good cauliflower from a poor one.

I even made some money for the school farm at parents' evenings where each parent had a five-minute appointment to discuss their child's progress.

I was very professional and talked about each student in detail but just as certain parents headed for the door I went, very casually, into my sales pitch.

'The school farm has some very nice produce to sell – plenty of eggs and vegetables – can I interest you?'

At one parents' evening I sold eight half-pigs for freezers worth £300 in total, plus twelve dozen eggs and ten trays of bedding plants.

Keeping The School Farm Up And Running

One very good customer, Mrs Parsons, said 'Mr Terry, you haven't left me enough for my bus fare home.' As she left the classroom I was smiling.

At that moment Mr Beech walked along the corridor.

'Well you're looking pleased with yourself, have you had a worthwhile evening?'

'I have, Mr Beech, thank you, very rewarding,' I replied. Little did he know that I was one of the very few teachers in Britain who could chalk up a profit for his department at a parents' evening. However, it was in a very good cause and my conscience was crystal clear, although I had a shrewd idea that most of my students, staff and parents had got my enterprising ways weighed up.

A new music teacher, a Mr Mark Fielding, was appointed at the school and apparently, one day he was talking to Mr Clive Salt, one of the art teachers and telling him he was a keen tomato grower and needed some manure for his plants. Clive informed him that it was no use asking John Terry unless he was prepared to pay for it.

'But I only want a bucket full of sheep muck for my tomatoes,' Mark said 'I think it's better than Baby Bio.'

'Oh good grief,' Clive spluttered. 'Don't tell him that, the beggar will be charging Baby Bio prices if you do.'

It's funny but Mark never did ask me for that bucket of sheep manure. I wonder why.

To help supplement funds, during the evenings I started to give more talks and after-dinner speeches, telling some anecdotes about the school farm. These talks were very much enjoyed by the listeners and they showed their appreciation by buying some of the eggs and things I had taken along. On some occasions the groups gave a donation to help boost the school funds and buy feed for the animals. I was going down very well and in great demand until one evening when I was booked to give a talk to a very upmarket ladies group in Leamington Spa.

I had to wear my dinner jacket to attend. That was the sort of evening it was. I found the hotel and parked my car. I entered the hotel and found the function room where the event was taking place. As I walked through the door a lady almost pounced on me and said very haughtily, 'Who are you and what do you want?'

'I'm your guest speaker,' I replied, feeling quite put out and thinking it was a very poor way to treat your guests.

After the dinner I had planned to show them some colour slides of the school farm. I was introduced and I did a five-minute introductory talk before starting the slide show.

'I'm ready to show the slides now so could we have the lights out please?' I asked.

The lights were switched off, the curtains drawn and the room went completely black. You couldn't see a thing, it was like the black hole of Calcutta. As quick as a flash, in my rustic voice I said, 'I've always wondered what it was like for one of our rams to be let out in the same field as about fifty old ewes.'

It went down like a lead balloon. There was dead silence, not even the vestige of a titter. They made it quite clear they didn't regard it as very amusing at all. In fact I heard one lady say, 'He's awfully coarse, isn't he? I wonder where our secretary found him.'

After that remark I did my talk very quickly, editing it quite considerably along the way and made a hasty exit. I didn't sell many eggs to boost the funds that night.

The school open evening was an annual event, with the parents coming along to see the students' work displayed in the classrooms, artwork displayed in the entrance halls and dining room as well as examples of items made in the technology department. The home economics department had a 'taste in' where the parents could sample some of the food prepared by the students.

The school farm and gardens were always popular on these occasions, especially if it was a warm evening. To be fair to the students our gardens always look immaculate and our livestock were all on show. Projects and exercise books were placed in the mobile classroom for the parents to browse through. It was all very civilised and enjoyable. Now that finances were a problem I decided that, as well as the educational aspect we could turn this into a commercial enterprise. We were open for business.

Peter, Robert, Linda and Gillian worked hard to set up a plant stall selling geraniums and fuchsias that we had grown from cuttings. We had trays of bedding plants such as alyssum and lobelia and also some hanging baskets all planted up and ready to hang. The mothers loved these.

Jason, Louise, Jonathon, Michael and Angela showed their expertise handling the livestock and answered questions put to them while they showed the parents our cattle, sheep, pigs, goats, rabbits, guinea pigs, hens, ducks and geese. I could see the parents were impressed by the knowledge they showed.

Oliver, Matthew, James, Kathryn, Claire and Sue organised competitions such as how many sweets in the jar or guess the weight of the lamb. There was a lot of fun and laughter and our evening in particular was a great success.

The school itself also put on some competitions to help general school funds – this produced only a modest income. I did hear that Mr Beech was a little upset because the school farm seemed to take most of the parents' money thus leaving them with less to spend on the school in general. In fact, Mr Beech openly declared that the school farm had taken three times the amount as the rest of the school. I don't think he was too pleased about that.

Chapter Ten
Community Spirit And Too Much Barley

Warwickshire County Council had some money in their funds for projects for the community. After a meeting with Mr Beech it was agreed that I should try to make the school farm available to more members of the public in the form of groups and societies visiting the farm. These groups could include Women's Institutes, Townswomen's Guilds and Young Farmers' Clubs to name but three, but perhaps most of our visits would be from students of other schools on organised visits.

After a lot of form filling and a meeting with Warwickshire County Council officials, they agreed to help. However, they wouldn't give us money just to feed our animals – we had to ask for something specific that would benefit our school farm and the community. After a great deal of thought I decided to ask for a new animal house.

They agreed to this just as long as I used the new animal house and the school farm for members of the community and had members of the community in to look at and learn about livestock and the environment and also make use of our gardens. I agreed to these terms and suggested we set up a picnic area.

I drew up some plans and then contacted three agricultural construction firms to give me estimates. All three quotations were similar in price but then one firm, Whittles, telephoned me with a very good suggestion.

'George Wimpole here,' said a voice on the telephone. 'We have got a demonstration building standing idle at the Royal Showground at Stoneleigh. We constructed it just before the show so it is only about three months old.'

'That sounds interesting. Does that mean it won't be quite as expensive as a brand new one?' I asked, at the same time getting ready to do some bartering.

'Yes Mr Terry, it does. We will look after you, since you represent a school. I think it's marvellous having a school farm, I wish they'd had one when I was at school.'

I agreed to meet him that evening at the Royal Showground at 5.30pm. I thought I would strike while the iron was hot because it sounded ideal.

The building on offer turned out to be an excellent steel-framed structure measuring thirty feet by thirty feet and standing ten feet to the eaves. The top half was clad with Yorkshire boarding, the bottom half was timber, and it had a good, strong metal ten-foot gate. The company would dismantle it and erect it on our site for £1200, which was a very fair price indeed. I agreed to have it. George Wimpole gave me the plans which I submitted to the local council. Surprisingly the plans were passed first time.

Our large wooden building at school was past its best and needed to be knocked down and the new building erected in its place. It was summer so most of our stock was outside and we had always got our brick building to fall back on if we wanted to bring any of our animals inside.

Mr Beech and I both agreed it was too dangerous for my students to be climbing about on roofs wielding sledgehammers so it was demolished by our two caretakers Ivan and Keith, much to our students' disappointment.

All of this brought back memories of my first year of teaching. It was 1974 and I had asked Mr Beech for an old bicycle shed that the students didn't use. It was falling down anyway but I wanted to keep pigs in it. The idea horrified him.

'What on earth would the County Council think – me giving you a perfectly good bicycle shed – a shed they paid for to house bicycles in, not dirty pigs?' he said indignantly.

I took that to be a no.

My students were very disappointed that they could not have the shed so, when no one was looking, including me, half of the front and half of the back disappeared. When Mr Beech spotted it he said 'Oh, it really is an eyesore isn't it? Quite a shambles' He then gave us permission to move it.

We dismantled what was left of it and put it together on its new site and strangely enough the missing bits re-appeared. We had a good pig shed.

Our caretakers made an excellent job of taking down the

Community Spirit And Too Much Barley

old shed and two days after they completed this Whittles started putting up the new building. My students were so excited about all the changes. The new building was soon erected and to make it much better for both animals and visitors we employed another firm to concrete the floor and divide the building into five large pens, using bricks and breeze blocks, with a central feed passage. Finally, this firm made small wooden gates to fit each pen. It all looked wonderful. It looked too good to get dirty, however we soon moved our animals in.

'It looks fit for a queen,' said Eleanor with pride.

The weather was hot and Windsor Grand Good News and her Aberdeen Angus x Holstein-Friesian friend Rosie were out in the paddock next to the building. I was sitting at my desk in my mobile classroom after dismissing my class for the day and my student helpers had started to arrive. Out of the corner of my eye I saw Eleanor go into the paddock to look at the heifers. However, within minutes she burst into the classroom. Now I should have been quite used to pupils bursting in on me but every time it happened my heart went into reggae rhythm because I knew a trauma was about to develop.

Community Spirit And Too Much Barley

'Sir – Good News looks really poorly,' she gasped.
'What's the matter with her?'
'I don't know, she's lying down, she won't get up and she looks really off colour.'

I followed Eleanor out of the classroom to have a look for myself. She was right, sure enough Good News was lying down.

'Is she going to die, sir?' Eleanor asked in panic.
'I should jolly well hope not. Wait a minute, I haven't looked at her properly yet, calm down now,' I said, trying to keep calm myself.

Good News stood up after a bit of coaxing. She held her head down and forward, suggesting pain. Her back was arched up and she kept looking at her side. I could see she had stomach pains.

'She's got stomach ache but I can't think why.' Not another Harry the Hoover I thought pleadingly. I sat pondering for a minute.

'I bet she's eaten some litter – why do people drop litter?' I said sternly, not needing an answer. 'There are plenty of rubbish bins about. She could have started to lick a salty crisp packet and then just swallowed it or she could have eaten something much larger,' I surmised.

'Sir, I have just been in the new animal house and the big door was wide open, and I found the blue tub containing the rolled barley with its lid off and the tub on its side and sir, it's empty.'

I was very concerned to hear this and went to have a look, now closely followed by about a dozen very worried helpers.

'I was wrong about the litter,' I said. 'Look at those dirty hoof marks on the floor. Which idiot left that big door open?' I rounded on them. It went very quiet for a minute.

'I saw Lynne Robinson walking about the school farm this morning when she should have been in lessons,' remarked Matthew who had just joined us.

'Yes, I saw her too, we were both in a science lesson and we could see her through the window – she seemed to be creeping about,' agreed Stephen.

Matthew and Stephen had only recently come to help on the farm. Both wanted to work with animals when they left school.

'Why didn't you tell me at lunch time?' I asked.

'Well it was obvious she wasn't going to her lessons so we didn't want to tell tales,' said Stephen.

'She's a very unreliable girl and I bet she won't even remember she has left the door open, it just wouldn't occur to her that anything could go wrong,' I said.

'She is a bit slow, sir. In Mrs Clarke's lesson Mrs Clarke asked her what an Urdu was and she said it was what an urdresser gives you,' remarked Stephen.

'I'm not surprised,' I said.

'Yes, sir, and in Mr Martin's maths class Mr Martin asked her if you cut a banana into ten pieces, an apple into four pieces and a pear into two pieces what do you get? And she said a fruit salad, sir!' said Matthew. By this time the two boys were nearly in hysterics.

'I'm still not surprised,' I said.

I went back and had another look at Good News. She was still standing. I walked gently behind her and drove her slowly towards the new animal house. She went in, followed by the little black heifer called Rosie, who was making worried little noises. Good News lay down again. it was comfortable for her in there – she had some nice clean straw to lie on and it was warm for her.

'She's obviously eaten all the barley in the tub – I think Rosie is all right – Good News is the boss so fortunately Rosie wouldn't get a look in.'

'What happens now then?' asked Matthew.

'The barley will ferment in her rumen – that is her first stomach.'

'Yes, cows have four stomachs, the rumen, the reticulum, omasum and abomasum,' Eleanor explained correctly.

'Well done, Eleanor,' I said. 'I will go to the school office and telephone the vet now.'

'Could we lose her?' asked Eleanor who was running by my side.

'It's certainly possible – but we'll do everything we can to

Community Spirit And Too Much Barley

save her.'

I quickly went into the school office and, would you believe it, the school secretary Mrs Loveridge was using the telephone – she often used about a hundred words where a few would suffice. I didn't want to appear rude but at the same time my call was urgent. It was easy to tell when Mrs Loveridge had dialled a wrong number because she would only talk for ten minutes. She certainly knew how to make calls, she just didn't know how to end them.

At last she finished. I telephoned the vets' but it was engaged. I tried again and got through to the receptionist.

'Hold the line please I'll put you through to Simon,' she said.

Simon was one of the partners at the large veterinary practice. I told him what had happened to Good News.

'All right John, I'll be out to look at her within the next half hour, in the meantime you can start treatment.'

'What shall I do?'

'You need to place a heaped tablespoonful of bicarbonate of soda in a jug of water – mix it up then get it down her as fast as you can.'

'Yes all right, I'll do it straight away.' All the while I was thinking I would have to buy some bicarbonate of soda because we certainly didn't keep any in stock.

I got back to the farm in double quick time.

'Who has got a bike?' I asked anxiously.

Three or four students had come to school on bikes but I chose Jonathon simply because he was standing next to me.

I stuffed a £5 note into his hand and told him what I wanted. My sense of urgency must have transmitted itself pretty well because he ran like the wind for his bike and was soon speeding off on his errand. While he had gone I found our drenching bottle – an old wine bottle with a long neck. I washed it out and also a jug that really belonged to Miss Perrin from the home economics department.

Jonathon seemed to be gone ages but in reality it was only about ten minutes before he came racing back with the bicarbonate of soda. After mixing it up and putting it in the bottle Eleanor held Good News and I placed the bottle in the heifer's mouth, putting the bottle right to the back of her throat. I pulled her head back and the liquid soon disappeared down her throat. While I was doing this I explained to my students that the barley she had swallowed would make her stomach acid and the bicarbonate of soda would help balance the pH making the acid more alkaline. I was pleased I had completed the job before the vet arrived.

'What will the Queen say?' asked Matthew.

'She doesn't know yet,' I replied. I thought silently to myself: and she's not going to know.

We had kept Crystal for a good eight years but she had died recently. If Good News died in the same year it would not look good. We would stand no chance of getting another heifer from the Royal Farms – in fact they might finish with us altogether. I started to worry and wished the vet would hurry up and arrive.

The waiting seemed longer than it actually was. Simon got out of his car and took his stethoscope and various bottles and bags out of the boot. He examined Good News, listening to her heart and stomach or rumen through his stethoscope.

'Yes. I think she will be all right – her rumen is still working. I have seen much worse cases, perhaps she hasn't eaten as much barley as you thought.'

'I'm not sure how much was in the tub,' I said. 'And my students are not really sure either,' I added.

'This sounds like good news,' said Eleanor brightly.

'No, this is Good News,' Jonathon replied, pointing to the heifer.

My students were a lot happier now and so was I.

'Come and stand here and I'll explain what is happening,' said Simon.

The students gathered closely round him to listen, after all, this man knew more than Mr Terry did.

'Once the barley was swallowed it went into the rumen or first stomach where it was fermented by bacteria. This produced acid conditions and the contents of the rumen turned sour. The wall of the rumen can become inflamed, toxins will then be absorbed which could damage her liver. In this case I don't think she has eaten enough to die. She will pass out a lot of undigested barley in her faeces in about twenty-four hours time which will stink. She won't feel like eating for a day or two. Those are the signs to look out for.'

'What's the treatment?' asked Eleanor.

'The treatment will be quite easy. I will inject her with Finadyne, an anti-inflammatory drug and she also needs some more bicarbonate of soda and some antibiotics and some B vitamins.'

''I have got some antibiotics in stock.' I said.

Simon checked the ones I had which were penicillin. These proved to be fine and he told me to inject her for the next three to five days.

'That's all – just keep your eyes on her.' He washed his hands and went to his car. 'If she deteriorates call me and I will be back,' he said just before driving off.

My students fed and watered the other livestock and we checked Good News before leaving. I checked her twice that evening and twice during the night. Next morning she was much brighter.

During registration I sent for Lynne Robinson. Without an argument she admitted to missing her lessons and later admitted to hiding on the school farm. However, she couldn't remember leaving the door open, which was what I had predicted.

There was no point in losing my temper with her but I calmly explained the damage she had done. I sent her off to her head of year – Mr Searle, no doubt he would give her a detention and send a letter home to her parents. I made a note to see him to make sure she had reported to him.

Good News had totally recovered after forty-eight hours. We moved the barley tub so that no animals could get to it. Yes I admit it. It was shutting the stable door after the horse had bolted but at least we knew it would never happen again.

What a fright she had given us.

Chapter Eleven
The Royal Visit

It had been a rush-rush day all round. I had snatched a quick lunch and then met some of my students in the school garden to get some weeding done before afternoon lessons started. Work was going well.

'What are these flowers called?' asked Gillian.

'They are called Kniphofia or red hot pokers to give them their common name,' I replied.

'My grandad crossed some of those with some forget-me-nots,' said Peter cheekily.

'Peter, that is not botanically possible – but do tell,' I replied. I knew I was being set up.

'Yes sir, he did. He came up with a painful reminder.'

I had to laugh and then a smart-looking year eight student appeared.

'He's not a gardener,' observed Peter. 'He's too tidy.'

The lad heard but chose to ignore the remark and turned to me.

'I've got a message for you, sir.'

'Come on then, out with it, what is it?'

'Mr Beech wants to see you in his office immediately, sir.'

'Oh yes? What have you done, sir?' asked Robert.

I ignored him. It was best when they were in that mood.

'He sent for me on Wednesday,' continued Robert, determined to press the issue.

'What had you done this time?' I asked as I made my way towards Mr Beech's office.

'Nothing. Except for being late.'

'Well you should get up earlier shouldn't you?'

'I will sir but I call Mr Beech "Musketeer" now.'

'Why?' I asked but should have known better.

'He says I musketeer for five to nine. You'll be all right sir. Mind you, it depends what mood he's in – it depends if he has had his lunch. Before lunch he grumbles and after lunch he has indigestion.

'It will be good news,' I said firmly. 'Why do you always look on the pessimistic side?'

I didn't have time for the answer, within minutes I was in Mr Beech's office.

'I have been informed by Warwickshire County Council that Her Majesty Queen Elizabeth II and His Royal Highness the Duke of Edinburgh would like to come and visit,' he announced.

'Oh' was all I could say as my jaw dropped open.

'Yes. It appears they want to see the new heifer – what do you call her? In her new home.'

'She's called Windsor Grand Good News,' I said proudly.

'Ah, well Mr Terry, they would like to meet your students, yourself and see the school farm.'

Now although I feigned surprise this announcement didn't really come as a complete shock because I had recently received a letter from the Royal Farm manager asking how Good News was settling in and at the end of the letter it said: 'I expect you will be preparing for Her Majesty's visit to your school.'

I didn't think it was a joke but at the same time I thought he had got his facts wrong. I almost telephoned him to ask but decided against it. I just waited.

'Don't say anything to anybody yet Mr Terry,' continued Mr Beech. 'I will announce it at tomorrow morning's briefing. Everything will have to be painted of course,' he added as I walked towards the door.

'Everything?' I queried.

'Yes, everything, even that heifer of yours if she looks dirty.'

The announcement was made in the staff briefing the following morning. It was mid-July, we were soon to break up for the summer holidays and the Queen and Duke of Edinburgh would visit us on Thursday 8 December 1994.

Mr Beech announced it to the whole school in morning Assembly. At morning break my students ran over to the school farm to see if I had more details and to confirm that it was true. They were so excited they could hardly believe it.

The Royal Visit

That evening Mr Beech visited us on the farm to see what painting needed doing. This made a change because he usually only turned up when there was a problem like a bad smell or a life-threatening crisis.

We looked in the new animal building first, it was brand new so there was little to be done there.

Our brick-built animal building certainly needed some attention. The walls needed painting white both inside and out with all doors to be painted green with black hinges.

All the paving slabs at the rear of the classroom would need re-laying as we didn't want Her Majesty to catch her toe on the uneven slabs and fall flat on her face. The fish pond and duck pond would need cleaning out while the large pile of manure at the rear of the pig pen would have to be removed and taken to another farm out of 'smell's' way.

Two poultry runs would need fixing and we needed to purchase more tubs and containers to fill with plants. Life in the classroom could not be disrupted so most of these jobs would have to be done before and after school and at weekends.

After Mr Beech had finished his tour I said 'Our farm funds are very low, perhaps the school fund will pay for all this maintenance. Please?'

'Yes, I understand that Mr Terry – get whatever you need.'

I nearly fainted from shock. This was music to my ears - the Queen and Duke of Edinburgh should visit more often.

'What about things like paintbrushes and turpentine?' I asked. I knew I was pushing my luck but why not? It's not every day Royalty visit you.

'Yes Mr Terry. Get whatever you need and the school fund will reimburse you.'

Eleanor, who had started it all, had just left school to go on and be a student at the Sixth Form College. I telephoned her with the exciting news. She was overjoyed.

'Is that right? Well I never. When I wrote the letter with the other students telling the Queen that Crystal had died, then asking for another heifer and finally inviting her to visit I thought to myself – well I might get a letter back in reply but I never dreamt there would be an actual visit.'

'You've done very well – without your letter to the Queen there wouldn't be a Royal visit. We've got a lot to thank you for,' I said.

'Will I get to meet her?' she asked.

'I should think you will be top of the list,' I replied.

Meanwhile, back in my classroom my students could not stop talking about it.

'Will I have to talk in a posh accent?' asked Jonathon.

'You've got a terrible accent. If I were you I wouldn't talk at all,' replied Robert sarcastically before adding, 'you could do with elocution lessons.'

'No need. I can change a light bulb and wire a plug,'

The Royal Visit

Jonathon replied, taking the sting out of Robert's remarks.

After the long summer holiday was over painting the brick building inside and out was our first big job.

School funds paid a firm to re-lay the slabs at the rear of the classroom. It was a great help as we really hadn't got the time to do this job – we were good at it mind – my students and myself over the years had laid over 500.

The school farm and gardens always looked good but now it all looked wonderful. Time was flying by and the visit which at one time had been months away was now rapidly approaching.

Our last task was to mount a display and the mobile classroom next door to mine was the obvious place. It was only used for a few lessons per day. I negotiated with the staff who taught in there and they agreed to find alternative accommodation on the day before the visit and the day of the visit. Everyone co-operated marvellously.

On the tables we placed examples of students' work on many projects. We set up display boards with photographs showing how the department had looked in 1974 – an acre of wilderness. We then put many more photographs showing how the department had developed. All the prize certificates and 700 rosettes won by the sheep and cattle were also put on display.

The day before the visit the whole school had a rehearsal with Mr Beech playing the part of the Duke of Edinburgh. Rehearsal day was on a Wednesday but we changed to Thursday's timetable to get things absolutely perfect. The schedule had been written down and every student and every member of staff knew exactly where they were to be and even where to stand on the playground. Timing was to military standards – all organised by Mr Bell, the deputy headmaster.

The evening before the visit we checked everything again on the school farm. The animals had all been cleaned out, all the painting had been done, paving slabs had been relaid, both ponds had been cleaned, the manure pile had been taken away, poultry runs were fixed and we had more tubs and containers filled with plants than we had ever had before – we even had flower arrangements.

The whole school would see the Queen and Duke of Edinburgh and a few of us would actually speak to her. They would spend about twenty minutes with me which was a great honour.

When the Queen meets performers at such events as the Royal Variety Show she shakes hands with them and says a few words then moves on to the next person in line. I would get a lot more attention than that.

I went over the final plans with my students, they all knew where to stand and which animals were under their care.

'Robert, don't be late,' I said sternly.

'No sir, I won't.'

'Incidentally, I saw you leaving Mr Beech's office this morning, was he telling you off for being late again?'

'Yes, sir.'

'And what excuse did you give this time?' I asked.

'As you know, sir, we have to drive along the new bypass to get to school.'

'Yes I know that,' I replied.

'Well sir, a lorry carrying glue had tipped over.'

'Was anyone hurt?'

'No sir, but we all had to stick to the inside lane.'

I laughed. I couldn't help it.

'Come to think about it, I saw you arriving at school in a brand new sports car – so you shouldn't be late,' I said.

'Yes sir, but I arrive late much faster now!'

'Oh go and sit down,' I said.

Sarah, our head girl arrived at my classroom door.

'Hello Sarah,' I said cheerfully.

'Hello sir. Mr Beech says I'm to present the Queen with a posy of flowers when she arrives tomorrow morning.'

'That is a great honour,' I said.

'I know sir, but what do I say to her?'

'Good morning Your Majesty, welcome to our school.'

'Thank you sir. By the way, what does ER stand for?' she asked.

'Elizabeth Regina,' I said.

The Royal Visit

'Well can't I just say "'ere ya, ER?"'

'No you most certainly cannot,' I said emphatically.

The night before the visit I slept very badly. Not only were my nerves on edge but it was blowing a gale and the wind howled and moaned all night.

Next morning I was up before the birds and arrived at school very early to give Good News her final wash and brush up.

Security was at the school gate checking us all in and a helicopter hovered overhead. Fortunately the black clouds had started to clear. It had rained very hard during the night but was now just beginning to move away.

The sniffer dogs and handlers were already in school. The Springer spaniels were doing a thorough job, keen and enthusiastic they snuffled about everywhere.

Security officers however, were not happy with a cupboard in the drama department which contained toy guns. They were immediately confiscated for the day just in case someone took it into their heads to play silly beggars and stage a wild west routine.

We fed the livestock and then I marked the register.

'I see you've got your suit on, sir,' remarked Louise.

'You look good enough to meet the Queen, sir,' quipped Angela.

'All right, go ahead, get it out of your systems,' I said.

I had other teachers taking my lessons for the whole morning so that I could concentrate on the visit. Eleanor came in very early. She had finished at our school so her school uniform was replaced with a smart cream blouse, black jacket and black skirt.

The dark clouds had by now broken up completely – it was a fine day and quite mild for the time of year. I could wear my suit without my coat on the top. I would feel more comfortable.

Banks of television crews and photographers arrived. The atmosphere was beginning to build up.

The Queen and Duke of Edinburgh arrived at the railway station on time and were welcomed by over 300 well wishers, many carrying banners and flags.

The royal train weighs twice the weight of a normal train due to its armour plating. Its eight coaches also carried the special staff. At the station they were welcomed by various dignitaries, including the Lord Lieutenant of Warwickshire, the Mayor, the Chairman of Warwickshire County Council and the Chief Constable for Warwickshire. This was the Queen's first visit to our town and everyone wanted to make it a memorable one.

The Rolls Royce Silver Phantom, with no number plates, then took the Royal party to our school.

Outside the school the streets were lined with hundreds of schoolchildren with their teachers who had abandoned lessons to get a glimpse of the Queen. We knew they were getting close by the cheers that went up from the roadside. I took a deep breath. This was it, this was what we had all been waiting for.

As the car entered our school gates and passed along the drive a resounding cheer echoed around the grounds. The Royal standard was flying proudly on top of our school.

At the front of the school the Queen was introduced to Mr Beech, the chairman of the board of governors, other governors, various staff, the head boy and Sarah, our head girl, presented the Queen with a posy of flowers.

The Queen then went to visit the language department where she spoke to the students in fluent French while the Duke of Edinburgh went to see students and staff involved in the Duke of Edinburgh Award Scheme, where he met past and present winners.

The two were then re-united outside our library where they listened to two original compositions and then chatted to members of the school music ensemble.

They then walked across the playground towards the school farm. The whole school lined both sides of their route, forming a guard of honour. The Queen and Duke of Edinburgh made a few brief stops to talk to the students and then right at the end of about 1,200 students and seventy staff stood me – a lone figure waiting for them in the entrance to the school farm.

The Royal Visit

I could see them steadily getting closer and my heart began to race.

The Queen is smaller than people realise, perhaps slightly smaller than me. She wore a wool, purple coat with matching wide brimmed hat, black shoes and carried a black handbag. She had a spectacular purple brooch pinned to her coat. The Duke was in a grey suit and they were being escorted by Mr Beech with lots of dignitaries and detectives following close behind. The detectives' eyes looked everywhere. My moment was quickly approaching. I felt great.

Mr Beech introduced me and I said, 'Good morning Your Majesty.'

'Good morning Mr Terry,' the Queen replied and I received my Royal handshake.

The moment I said 'Good morning Your Majesty' and the Queen replied is definitely the best moment of my school life. I don't think anything could ever overshadow that moment. There was certainly a tear of happiness in my eyes.

I welcomed her to the school farm. I explained that I was a former pupil at the school and that as I started teaching there in 1974 I had now completed twenty years on the staff.

I told her that I took over the acre of wasteland with only fifteen pupils taking the subject and over the years it had developed into our school farm. She looked at me all the time I was talking to her, smiling and taking a real interest. Mr Beech, I was pleased to see, melted into the background. I would have her attention for the next twenty minutes.

The first animals for her to see were two of our prize-winning Kerry Hill ewes. They had been shown all summer and they stood perfectly on their halters held by my students.

'What wonderful black and white markings. Have they won many prizes?' the Queen asked.

'One or two, Ma'am,' I replied modestly.

She went on to ask when we sheared them. I explained

they were sheared on Christmas Eve.

I sometimes think it's a bit harsh – shearing them at that time of year,' she said. 'Don't they get cold?'

I explained that they were kept indoors with plenty of straw and if it got very cold we gave them coats to wear.

The Queen was now walking by my side. I hadn't met the Duke yet – he was walking behind chatting to the youngsters.

We walked into our new animal house containing rabbits, guinea pigs, our British Alpine goats, Good News and her friend Rosie.

The Royal Visit

The Queen's eyes lit up when she saw Windsor Grand Good News. Eleanor and Jonathon put a halter on her and led her forward.

Both Eleanor and Jonathon said 'Good morning Your Majesty.' And the Queen responded with 'Good morning.'

Then, just as the Queen approached her Good News did something that made a magical moment: she bowed her head. The 'aahs' and 'oohs' that went up were unbelievable and in spite of Jonathon and Eleanor trying to explain later on that it was more the enticement of newly laid straw rather than a mark of respect it was no good, the magical moment was etched in everyone's minds.

The Queen's first question to Eleanor was 'Is Good News behaving herself?'

'She is Ma'am.'

'Now then, I think that you are both slightly nervous because I am here – there is no need to be. I can see you are not quite your usual selves because you have put the halter on a little tight and it is too near her eyes.'

'Oh yes, so it is, thank you,' replied Eleanor and Jonathon. My students were just about to put the halter on again when the Queen leaned over and adjusted the halter for them.

'There, that's better,' she said.

I was very impressed. I knew the Queen was used to animals, especially horses, but here she was getting involved with our animals – real 'hands-on' experience.

She asked the students what we fed her on and she asked about Good News's friend Rosie, our Aberdeen Angus x Holstein Friesian.

She then turned to me and asked, 'What bull are you going to use on Good News?'

Now 'use on her' was a real farming term. I could see some of the 'townie' cameramen were puzzled.

My reply was 'I am lucky Ma'am, because your farm manager has agreed that I use your new bull, Windsor Imperial December Boy.

'Oh, he will do a wonderful job on this heifer and I am sure you will have a lovely calf,' she replied.

Rabbits On Report

Now that was another real farming term that we farmers use – 'wonderful job'.

'She looks very fit and healthy, Mr Terry, it is nice to see that she is being well looked after and loved by your students.'

I was pleased I had got the Royal seal of approval. She then asked if the Royal Farms had looked after us. I said I couldn't speak highly enough of them and that they were excellent.

After this she turned to look at the goats. She did this as the Duke of Edinburgh walked in. I was introduced to him and we shook hands.

'Well it all looks wonderfully neat and tidy – a well-run farm – but I think you overdid the watering in the night.'

He was referring to the torrential downpour we had received. I know the Duke is noted for making controversial comments but he didn't make any to me.

'What breed are the goats?' he asked.

'British Alpine,' I said proudly.

'That's a contradiction in terms,' he said. Then he looked at Angela and Louise and explained: 'Of course, there are no British Alps.'

They were delighted to see our rabbits and guinea pigs and the Queen walked with me to the end of the building to look at our show rams, who looked outstanding – both were Royal Show prize winners – and I could see the Royal couple were very impressed.

Cameras were rolling and photographs taken all the time. I stood at the end of the building with the Queen. We stood with the wall behind us and a photograph was taken with just the two of us on it. I was looking forward to seeing that one when it was developed.

We then walked back outside closely followed by all the other important visitors including the Lord Lieutenant – himself a landowner.

We all looked at the other sheep, ducks on the pond and the chickens in their newly fixed runs.

We then all went into the classrooms to look at the displays. When Her Majesty walked into the room and saw all our rosettes she was open mouthed in amazement.

'I thought you said you had won one or two,' she said. 'You have done extremely well to win all these in open competition,' she added.

She was quick to spot the female championships and all the first prizes won at the Royal Show at Stoneleigh.

She looked at all of our photographs. She was particularly interested in the ones showing our pet fox cub Vicky. Vicky had been rescued as a cub and reared up at the school. The Queen asked if the cub had become very tame and I told her that Vicky was too tame to be released back into the wild and had gone to live on an animal sanctuary.

Both the Queen and the Duke of Edinburgh were impressed with the standard of work the students had produced – both classwork and projects.

They then left the classroom and went on to the science laboratories and then to plant a commemorative tree at the front of the school which would mark her visit.

Before they left the school farm I thanked them both for coming and they both thanked me.

I had done it, and so had my students.

I then walked up to the front of the school to watch as she planted an oak tree.

Mr Beech and the Warwickshire County Council officials said goodbye. The Queen and Duke got back into the Rolls Royce and were driven away to their next engagement which was a visit to our recently rebuilt local hospital.

We had certainly been honoured with the Royal visit. The last time our town had been visited by a reigning monarch was during the Second World War after the Blitz.

The Queen was very relaxed with me, natural and genuinely interested in the farm and she had an excellent knowledge of livestock. This visit placed the Royal seal of approval on our school farm and certainly raised our pride. It was a dignified visit – the very best day in the history of the school farm and the history of the school in general.

The visit, of course, followed Eleanor's letter. Eleanor had organised that letter with about twenty other students,

The Royal Visit

but without that letter the visit would never have gone ahead.

That evening we were on both the BBC and ITV which we enjoyed watching.

Many of the students, in years to come, would be able to tell their grandchildren about this day.

The photographs of the event were soon developed and printed. The Queen was smiling on all of them and the one with just her and myself is now one of my prize possessions and has pride of place on my kitchen wall.

After the visit was over I sent a thank you letter to Buckingham Palace and also enclosed my other two books 'Pigs In The Playground' and 'Calves in the Classroom'.

I then received the following letter from Buckingham Palace:

Dear Mr Terry,
The Queen has asked me to thank you for your very kind letter of 12 December and to say how much she enjoyed her visit to the school. Her Majesty was most grateful for the two books which you sent her. Unfortunately 'Ducks In Detention' which Eleanor sent to the Queen with her letter of 5 May seems to have been mislaid here and I wonder if you would be kind enough to send another copy so that the Queen can have a complete set.
Yours sincerely
Kenneth Scott.

Sir Kenneth Scott was Her Majesty's deputy private secretary. I sent off 'Ducks In Detention' and wrote 'To Your Majesty' inside it and I signed it.

I received another thank you letter as follows:-

Dear Mr Terry,
Many thanks for your letter of 10 January and for sending another copy of your book 'Ducks In Detention'. The Queen is delighted to have a complete set of these books.
Yours sincerely,
Kenneth Scott.

I still wonder, to this day how her original copy of 'Ducks In Detention' was mislaid. Had she loaned it to one of her grandchildren and they had not returned it? Or perhaps one of the Corgis had made off with it.

It's a wonderful feeling to know that the Queen has got all three books, in fact, it will be all four now because I have sent her a signed copy of this one.

Chapter Twelve
Our Rabbits Go Missing

Time went by and I managed to persuade a local engineering firm to sponsor us. They gave us a cheque for £250 to help with the feeding of our animals. It was a great boost to our funds and we were most grateful.

I had become even 'tighter' than ever. In fact one of my students, Carolyn, had told Mr Harris that, quote, 'Mr Terry is so tight with his money he even went into a card shop to see if they did Get Well cards on the NHS.'

'I'm not that bad,' I told Mr Harris.

'Oh no? Well there's a rumour going round that you've only just thrown your real Christmas tree away and let's face it John, it is nearly the end of June now.'

Mr Petty wasn't going to be left out.

'What's the difference between John Terry and a coconut?' he asked.

'No idea,' replied Harris.

'No, I don't know either but I'm sure you're going to tell us, aren't you?' I said.

'Well, you can get a drink out of a coconut,' Mr Petty enlightened us and they both roared with laughter.

'It's all very well laughing but my money-making plans are all in a good cause. I'm not going to lose the school farm without a fight,' I said seriously.

To justify our new animal house I needed to get the community involved with the farm and gardens. I had two visits organised, the local Women's Institute were coming for an afternoon visit and the County Goat Society were due on a Tuesday evening so I was hoping for two separate donations.

Desperately needing to get the other schools involved, I prepared a booklet describing our facilities and an encouraging letter asking them to visit our school farm. I could not charge a fee but Mr Beech agreed that I should ask for a donation. All money received would go towards the upkeep of our school farm.

I looked in the telephone directory and marked off all the local schools – first schools, middle, secondary and special. I then widened the net by picking out the more likely schools further afield.

The letters were duly sent out and I waited, impatiently, for the replies. The response was wonderful. Fifteen schools agreed to bring pupils along. A Mrs Morley, a teacher at a special school, wanted to bring a group of students aged around fifteen and sixteen. They didn't just want to look around the school but wanted to carry out tasks such as planting seeds in the greenhouse, planting out vegetable plants in the garden and helping get our sheep ready for shows – real hands-on experience. They wanted to come every Thursday morning for six weeks. I was free for two lessons on a Thursday morning so I could teach them and then leave them with their own staff while I taught my lessons. With a bit of juggling around everything fitted in very nicely and everyone was happy.

These visits proved very successful and rewarding to all concerned. The students had severe learning difficulties and some had physical disabilities as well but Mrs Morley and her team of helpers were a model of patience, totally committed to their work. The students proved to be very diligent and persevered with their tasks, letting nothing beat them. One of the students, Joanne, was terrified of the animals on her first visit, cringeing away from even the most gentle lamb but by the end of the second visit she had gained enough confidence and courage to stroke the goats and pick up and hold a guinea pig.

Another student, Amanda, was also a lot more confident on her second visit. I taught her to milk our goat Sarah. The look of pure delight on Amanda's face when she squirted the first drop of milk into the bucket was a joy to behold. It was only a small thing but it was the highlight of my week and I'm sure it was hers too.

Most of the replies we received were from first schools, the majority of these would be visits to look, stroke and feed the animals and then produce drawings and paintings of them. In amongst them was a letter from a middle school who wanted to bring thirty pupils on a coach visit. The pupils were aged nine and ten. Their headmistress, Miss Alice Pumfrett then telephoned me to arrange a visit for 2.30pm on Wednesday 12 – a fortnight away.

It would just mean me having a quick dinner and marking my register so that I would be ready to greet them. I had free periods for the whole of Wednesday afternoon and so I didn't have to worry about staff covering my lessons. I thought my farm helpers would jump at the chance to show these nine and ten year olds around and pass on the knowledge they had gained. I told them what I had in mind and nearly all of them were full of enthusiasm.

'Let's make it really good for them,' said Rebecca.

'Yes' said Edward. 'Let's do something for them.'

'What about putting some labels and information sheets on the animal pens,' said Rebecca excitedly.

This was great. I had wanted to do something along those lines myself but I hadn't mentioned it to them so that was really good. We were all on the same wavelength.

We set to and made some labels including 'British Alpine Goat. Name: Higham Sarah.' And then we produced a small information pack about Sarah and goats in general. Each animal was written about in turn – my students had a great time doing this, working in groups and using lots of felt-tipped pens, card and sticky-backed plastic. It looked like a set from 'Blue Peter'. Not only did it educate their minds academically this kind of work also taught them co-operation and how to work as a team, in harmony.

My students had to find out the information, summarise it and write it up. Best handwriting of course, and while they were doing that they were learning and doing something useful at the same time. All of this work was completed during lunchtimes. No way could I use biology or science lessons to do things like making these labels for the animals. I had to stick to the syllabus and not venture from it, there was no time to do or talk about other things. Life in the science department was far more rigid and inflexible, I had to be far more serious too. I did, however, perform a pickled onion scam.

Rabbits On Report

I had to teach a practical biology lesson on the structure and function of eyes. Sheep eyes, not from our pedigree sheep I hasten to add, were kept in the science department freezer. I took seven out of the freezer so they would thaw out for the following day.

I looked at the eyes sitting in their enamel dish and they looked back at me. Ugh! I then planned my lesson for the next day. I was well organised.

That evening I gave an after-dinner speech at the Rotary Club. It was a splendid meal with honey-roast gammon, roast fresh turkey, dressed salmon with various salads and hot potatoes. I placed two pickled onions on my plate. As guest speaker I was seated at the top table and was thinking about my forthcoming talk, hoping they would laugh in all the right places, when my mind began to wander to tomorrow's lesson on eyes. I looked down at my plate and those two pickled onions looked back at me and I'll swear one of them winked at me. They bore so much resemblance to the sheep's eyes it gave me an idea, one I couldn't resist. The students were always playing practical jokes on me – now it was payback time. Could I fool them?

Next day I rolled up to school armed with a jar of pickled onions. I fetched the seven eyes out of the 'prep room' and placed everything out of sight in my laboratory. I then went to see Miss Smithers, one of the art teachers.

'Can you let me have a paintbrush and some black, white and grey poster paint,' I asked.

'What on earth do you want those for?' she asked, taken aback.

'I'd rather not say at this stage,' I replied.

'Oh all right, Mr Secretive, suit yourself.' She went off to find the required items. When she came back she said, 'Of course you do realise that mixing black and white together will give you grey don't you.'

'Yes, but I haven't got time to fiddle about,' I replied and dashed off.

Time had beaten me as I had to go and supervise the feeding and looking after the animals. Then it was time for registration, then Mr Beech's Assembly and then lessons. At break time I continued with my artwork where no one could see what I was doing. I took the roundest pickled onion I could find, made sure it was the same size as the eyes and wiped the vinegar off with a towel. I then got to work painting it to resemble a sheep's eye – even though I say so myself it looked very realistic, I could hardly tell the difference. I only hoped I could when it came to the 'crunch'.

I now had eight eyes and I placed each one in a separate enamel dish. I hid them all under my bench. I had one lesson to take, then the 'eye' lesson just before lunch and if that didn't put them off their dinner nothing would. The lesson soon came around, the class walked in, sat down and I took the register as normal. I then called them to assemble around the front bench. They brought their stools with them and sat down.

I reminded them that during the last lesson we had looked in the textbooks at the different parts of the eye and found out what each part was for. I asked some questions to see how much they had remembered. It was then I brought out the eight dishes, each with one eye in it and put them in front of me. I told them that I would dissect one now and then working in groups they would dissect the others.

A few of them pulled a face and moaned but most watched me with enthusiasm, I asked them questions while I worked and we identified parts such as the lens and the optic nerve. I showed them where to cut with the scalpel and it all went well. They were very good and had remembered the theory work from the last lesson.

'Right then, I want you to get into groups to dissect these eyes but before you do, do you realise that in the middle eastern countries sheep's eyes are regarded as quite a delicacy and to tell the truth I can't resist one,' I said, looking longingly at the eyes. They all looked very puzzled. I quickly took the pickled onion 'eye' in my fingertips and held it up to my mouth.

'Mmm.' I savoured the moment then bit into it. It really crunched, then I chewed it around with a real satisfied smile.

Their faces were something I will never forget, there was both disgust and horror. I chewed it around and swallowed it.

The noise from them, including screams was very, very loud.

'Listen to the crunch,' I said as I took another bite.

'Oh for God's sake, sir,' said one boy as many more screams followed. Some students couldn't look. The noise was so great that Mr Adam Millerchip, teaching science next door, came in to investigate.

'What are you doing in here. Killing a pig?' he asked.

'Mr Terry's just eaten a sheep's eye,' replied one student in disgust.

Mr Millerchip beat a hasty retreat back to his laboratory. I put the last of the 'eye' in my mouth and told them they must not try to copy me.

'Don't worry. sir.'

'No way.'

'No chance.'

The rest of the lesson went as planned and they carried out their dissecting but as they left the classroom they made a few remarks.

'I still feel sick, sir.' And 'You've put me off my dinner, sir.'

I wondered how long it would take before the staff room was abuzz with John Terry's latest escapade.

I think it was about five minutes. I wasn't in the staff room but apparently Adam Millerchip went in and told the technology staff – who always sat in the same corner – that John Terry had eaten a sheep's eye.

At afternoon registration my students told their form teachers and it was the subject of conversation around everyone's tea table when they went home. The week progressed and students kept coming up to me asking, 'Did you really eat a sheep's eye, sir?'

I kept it going for exactly a week. My pupils were all sitting quietly wondering what to expect.

'I want you to bring your stools and come and sit around the front bench,' I said.

A chorus of protest went up.

'If you're going to eat sheep's eyes again you can forget it, I'm off' and 'I hope you're not going to eat anything again. Or 'What's on the menu this time?'

'Look, just come and sit down here all of you,' I instructed.

When they were settled I said, 'Remember the eyes?'

'Oh well sure, how could we forget. I think we'll remember that for the rest of our lives,' said Rebecca, turning to face the others. A chorus of agreement filled the air.

'Well here is one I prepared earlier,' I said in my best 'Blue Peter' voice, 'and here is one I am about to prepare.' I showed them the jar of pickled onions and the poster paint.

'You fraud, sir. You fooled us,' said one lad.

'I hear you are taking Jeremy Beadle's place on television next, sir.' Everyone laughed but I still heard one girl mutter 'Yes, but he still ate poster paint.'

In the meantime we were carrying on preparing for our visit from the middle school. My students enjoyed placing the information on the animal pens and they had tidied up the farm so everything looked good. I thought I had better do my bit so during the evenings I prepared a worksheet and farm trail for them to complete.

Mr Beech was very impressed, he was also pleased with all the hard work we had put in to make the school's visit a memorable one.

At this particular time we had two unruly students, Angela and Tracey. This was a different Angela to the one who had helped on the school farm. These two were fifteen years old and virtually out of control. Once again they had been placed on report for playing truant. 'On Report' meant they had to report to the teacher at the start of each lesson and give that teacher a form to fill in. The form was filled in at the end of the lesson. The member of staff would comment on behaviour, attitude and work completed and write in any homework set. Hopefully the student behaved, worked hard and learned their lesson.

Mr Beech told me that he was at his wit's end with these two girls. Not only were they truanting but they were in constant trouble with staff and had been caught bullying some of the younger, smaller students.

This unlikely pair wanted to work with children when they left school and Mr Beech suggested that they should be allowed to miss their lessons and help show our visitors around – perhaps his approval of them would improve their behaviour.

I didn't teach these two girls but perhaps I was fortunate in that respect, they were disruptive and had been known to swear at staff and also steal. I suggested that Angela and Tracey should come down to the school farm the day before the school visit to go through our plans. Next day two sulky faces arrived in my classroom.

'Now then, which one is Angela and which one is Tracey?' I asked.

'I'm Angela,' said one, chomping on gum, a habit I detest.

'Right, well get rid of your chewing gum,' I ordered.

'I'm Tracey,' said her equally sulky friend.

'If you've got chewing gum, bin it now,' I said.

Angela had blonde hair, she was very tall and slim, Tracey was shorter and plumper and both looked older than sixteen. They both wore very short skirts, another bone of contention with Mr Beech who was constantly battling with them to let the hems down. Apparently one of the staff was so fed up with them and the length of Tracey's skirt he told Mr Beech he could see everything except her Fallopian tubes – a remark to which Mr Beech took a very dim view and quite rightly said it was a very unprofessional thing to say.

I told the girls that they must behave and not let me down, or for that matter, the school or themselves – after all, the visitors would be made up of students and teachers. They both promised to be on their best behaviour and I believed them. I also added 'Anybody or indeed, anything that goes missing from this farm will be put on report.'

'Anybody or anything,' Angela repeated.

'Yes,' I said sternly.

We were well prepared and the next day Tracey spotted the coach carrying our visitors

'I wouldn't say it looks crowded but even the driver appears to be standing', said Angela with a cheeky grin.

The coach pulled into the car park, it stopped, the door opened and out spilled about thirty youngsters, boys and girls of various shapes and sizes. They walked towards us accompanied by their teachers, helpers and the coach driver.

Our Rabbits Go Missing

'Is it all right to leave the coach there?' he asked.

'Yes, It's quite all right there.'

'I bet he only became a coach driver so he can tell people where to get off,' Angela said quietly to me so that no one else could hear.

'All right Angela, not now, we haven't got the time.'

My farm helpers had been excused from their lessons and I introduced them and myself to the visitors. The teacher in charge was Miss Jane Tate. She was blonde, small, slim and very enthusiastic. She looked at Angela and said 'Hello, what's your name?'

'Angela, Miss.'

'That's a good name and are you a little angel?'

I said nothing.

I asked all the visitors to go into the classroom first where they sat down.

'I'm not going to talk for very long as I know you're all keen to see the animals and look around but there are one or two things I think I should tell you first.

I did a quick introduction and then asked 'Are there any questions?'

'Have you got any camels?' asked one little girl seriously.

'No,' I replied, thinking there's always one, and I realised with some of these children we had to go back to basics.

We then sorted the middle school children into groups of three, we had nearly as many helpers as visitors. We gave out the work sheets and farm trails.

Each group would start at a different part of the farm and then work round in rotation. There was plenty to see: our new heifer Windsor Grand Good News, her friend Rosie the black heifer, pedigree Kerry Hill sheep, pedigree British Alpine goats, pigs, rabbits, guinea pigs, hens, ducks and geese as well as our well-stocked fish pond, gardens and greenhouses.

I circulated around the groups and tried to keep an eye on everything when suddenly I heard a splash. I looked around to see that one boy had slipped and one of his legs had almost disappeared in the duck pond. He had not quite fallen in but his leg was submerged. He quickly pulled it out and the rest of his group laughed. The sounds of the laughter soon spread and other students from all over the farm and gardens came running up to the pond to laugh as well – they were quite cruel. It was embarrassing for the lad who by this time was close to tears and, of course his shoe, sock and trouser leg were wringing wet. Jane Tate was a little more sympathetic.

'What can I do, Miss?' he wailed.

'Well Thomas, take your shoe and sock off, we can dry your sock on the fence, drain the water out of your shoe and squeeze as much water as possible out of your trousers. The sun will soon dry you out.'

'Is that all?'

'Yes, I can't have you running around with no trousers on. Come on the rest of you, back into your groups, show's over.' And that was her last word on the matter.

Time went by very quickly, the children asked lots of sensible questions and most worksheets and farm trails were fully completed. Angela and Tracey had excelled themselves. I had watched them with the children and they were very good with them. To finalise we went back into the classroom.

'Who has enjoyed themselves?' I asked.

Thirty hands shot up in the air including Thomas with his wet trouser leg. The afternoon had been a great success.

'We want animals at our school,' shouted out one of them.

'Yes, we want some Dutch rabbits. They are lovely,' said another.

Jane looked quite embarrassed.

'Come on Miss, we want some animals at our school,' shouted yet another.

I noticed there was no mention of camels.

'We haven't got the facilities,' Jane replied and changed the subject rather quickly.

Jane then thanked my helpers and myself and I thanked them for coming. Jane then gave us a donation of £25 to help feed the animals so I thanked her again. The children then gave us three rousing cheers.

'Right' I said, 'you've got five minutes left so you can go back outside and look at your favourite animals again. There was a mass stampede for the door, they couldn't wait to get outside again. The five minutes was soon up and they all clambered back on to the coach and were gone.

'Will you tell Mr Beech that we've been good?' asked Tracey.

'I certainly will. Why can't you be like that all the time? Both you and Angela have been excellent and you've certainly got a way with children. I'm sure you'll have a happy and successful career working with them.'

'Thank you, sir, we loved it. Can we help you again when there are some more children to take round?' asked Angela.

'Yes. I'm sure of that,' I replied. 'So why are you two so often badly behaved?' I asked.

'School's boring. Most of these subjects are of no interest to us,' Tracey replied while Angela nodded in agreement. 'I've never liked school, sir. Even as a small child my own mother and father warned other children not to play with me,' she continued.

'Since I was eleven my parents have begged me to run away from home sir,' pitched in Angela with a smile.

'Now I'm quite sure neither of you is as bad as that.'

'No sir, not really we're not as black as we're painted but, sir, school is over for the day now so we would like to stay and help you and your regular helpers feed the animals if we may,' said Tracey.

'Well of course you may.'

My farm helpers would now get changed into working clothes and start to feed and water the animals. I was talking to a couple of my students outside my classroom door when suddenly Louise and Michael came running towards me.

'Sir, sir. Two of the Dutch rabbits have gone. They must have got out of their hutch, they're not there.'

'Are you sure?'

'Yes sir. Positive. They're not there.'

'All right, start looking for them. They can't have gone far.'

The rabbit hutches were placed in the animal house so I followed them into the building. The large rabbit hutch was definitely empty. Perhaps one of our visitors or one of my helpers had accidentally left the hutch door open.

These were two of our special Dutch rabbits, black and white ones with excellent markings; they were our best show specimens and I didn't want to lose them.

'We should find them quite soon. I bet they are still in the building somewhere. Look in all the corners,' I said.

We started moving bales of hay and straw and sacks of feed, being careful not to crush or injure any rabbit taking refuge behind them. I was surer we would find them quickly. Jason looked in one of the guinea pig hutches.

'Someone might have put them in here, sir,' he suggested, before shouting 'Sir, the two guinea pigs are not here either.'

'Was the hutch door shut?' I asked.

Our Rabbits Go Missing

'Yes, sir. I had to open it.'

'Someone's messing about here,' I exclaimed sharply. We carried on looking, then Jonathon came dashing up.

'Sir, three baby chickens have disappeared from the chicken run outside,' he said in alarm.

'I can't believe this,' I said but alarm bells were ringing in my head.

'Sir, someone must be messing about, this isn't by chance, three different types of animals would not just go missing,' said Michael.

'I quite agree Michael.'

We carried on looking but the rabbits and guinea pigs were certainly not in the animal building. Then we had to start searching outside. We found nothing. Not a trace, not a clue, and that was after a good half-hour.

Then the school secretary Mrs Loveridge came running over.

'Mr Terry. Mr Terry' she gasped. 'A headmistress from a middle school, Miss Alice Pumfrett, has just telephoned to say that unfortunately some of their pupils had actually smuggled two rabbits, two guinea pigs and three baby chicks back to their school.'

'Oh thank goodness for that.' I heaved a sigh of relief. 'At least we know the animals are all safe.'

'Yes Mr Terry, they are all quite safe and Miss Tate, is it? She has found some cardboard boxes to put them in and she is returning the animals to the school this very minute,' said Mrs Loveridge.

We all breathed a lot more easily and tried to see the funny side. The animals were safe and on their way back to us and we were all happy about that.

'Thank you very much, Mrs Loveridge.' I said.

'I've told you before Mr Terry, it's a farm secretary you need.'

I thanked her again and she returned to her office, leaving us to get on with our work, or rather our waiting.

We all stood around smiling and some students were laughing at what the children had done.

'Sir, you said that anybody or anything that goes missing

Rabbits On Report

from this farm will be put on report. Your words, sir' Angela said mischievously.

'Yes Angela, I did say that,' I replied.

'Well sir. Those lovely prize-winning rabbits went missing from this farm so does that mean they will be put on report?'

I smiled but before I could say anything Angela said, 'Rabbits on report, Mr Terry – now there is a novelty.'